CO

SCOT

WHISKY

Carol P. Shaw

HarperCollins*Publishers*

HarperCollins Publishers
Westerhill Rd, Bishopbriggs, Glasgow G64 2QT

www.fireandwater.com

First published 1996
Second edition 2000

Reprint 10 9 8 7 6 5 4 3 2 1 0

ISBN 0 00 472497 6

A catalogue record for this book is available from the British Library

Printed and bound in Italy by Amadeus S.p.A.

Contents

Scotch

Irish

Scotch

The History of Scotch Whisky-making

*I*t is widely accepted that whisky has been distilled in Scotland for hundreds of years, and different hypotheses as to its origins have been suggested. Some state that it was brought into the country by missionary monks from Ireland; others point out that, as the Arabs were among the first to learn distillation techniques, knights and men returning from the Crusades could have brought the knowledge back with them. It may well be, however, that it evolved simply as a means of using up barley which would otherwise have been ruined after a wet harvest.

The name itself is derived from the Gaelic, *uisge beatha*, meaning 'water of life'. The Latin equivalent, *aqua vitae*, was a term which was commonly used throughout Europe to describe the local spirit. *Aqua vitae* made its first appearance in official Scottish records in 1494, with the record of malt being sold to one Friar

John Cor with which to make the spirit, but *uisge* seems to have first been mentioned in the account of the funeral and wake of a Highland chieftain around 1618. The amount of whisky making throughout Scotland increased greatly during the seventeenth century, and nowhere more so than in the Highlands. In fact, so enthusiastic was the growth in distillation that before the end of the sixteenth century there had already been complaints in Parliament that so much barley was being used in whisky production that it was in short supply as a foodstuff! These distillers' method was basic and simple: a sack of barley might be soaked in water – for example, in a burn – for a day or two, then the barley would

be spread out in a dry place, allowing it to sprout, for around 10 days. The sprouting would be halted by drying the barley over a peat fire (peat being used as the main source of fuel in the Highlands). It was then put in a container with boiling water and yeast, to ferment. This mix would be passed twice through a pot still, emerging as whisky at the other end. These distillers had to be fairly skilled at their job, to possess the judgement to know when to take off the middle cut of the spirit (the drinkable part), avoiding the poisonous foreshots, at the start of the distillation, and the lower-quality feints, or aftershots, at the end. Although they had no instruments, methods did evolve of testing the whisky's strength, including setting fire to the spirit to measure the amount of liquid left behind, and mixing it with gunpowder to see how it reacted when ignited – if the gunpowder-and-whisky cocktail exploded, it was known that the whisky was too strong!

It was during the seventeenth century, too, that the first tax on whisky was introduced by Parliament, because of the pressing need to raise revenue to finance the army fighting in the English Civil War in 1644. Although it was reduced under the Commonwealth, this episode effectively marked the beginning of the principle of the taxation of whisky.

The union of Scotland and England in 1707, however, heralded some changes for the whisky industry, and few of them were constructive. A malt tax was introduced in 1725 which adversely affected the quality of beer – until then the most popular drink – and of whiskies produced by the professional commercial distillers in the more populous Lowlands, who were obliged to produce whiskies of poorer quality, with less malted barley content. These taxes also applied to Highland malt whisky, but in that still-inaccessible region it was much easier to ignore, and illicit distillation continued to flourish. This attempt at revenue raising, affecting the Lowland distillers but ignored in the Highlands, set a pattern for the rest of the century.

Sir Edward Landseer's somewhat romanticised view of an illicit still in the Highlands (United Distillers)

The large distillers in the Lowlands continued successfully to produce rough grain whisky whose quantity was more important than its quality, for consumption locally and in England, where it was often used as a basis for cheap gin. However, pressure from the English distillers, who were being undercut by Scottish imports flooding the market, encouraged Parliament to introduce a series of increasingly draconian taxes against the Scots whisky. The small distillers in the Highlands – most of whom were probably farmers and crofters, pursuing a lucrative sideline – continued to make superior quality whisky without paying tax. Much of this whisky was brought to the Lowlands for sale, where it was more popular with those who could afford it than the rougher spirit produced by the Lowland distillers. The government in London had no answer to the problems they had helped create in the whisky industry, other than to raise taxes still further, making the law seem more and more ineffectual.

Finally, however, pressure on the government brought an abandonment of its futile attempts at taxation and regulation. A Royal Commission was set up to investigate the industry, the Excise service in the Highlands was strengthened, and in 1822 an act was passed which brought harsher penalties for those found to be operating unlicensed stills. The following year the Excise Act made an attempt to encourage licensed distilling, cutting both duty and restrictions on exports to England. Now, an annual licence of £10 was introduced on stills over forty gallons (smaller stills were not allowed), and a more modest duty of 2/3d per gallon of whisky brought in. The Duke of Gordon, whose estates included the Glenlivet area, was a prime mover in the reforms, and he encouraged his tenants, including George Smith, producer of the whisky which came to be known as The Glenlivet, to take out licences. The new act was effective and successful, and the amount of legally distilled whisky consumed had risen threefold by 1827.

Freed from its legislative shackles, the whisky industry was able to concentrate on the development of its product and markets. The product itself was given an impetus by the invention by Aeneas Coffey, an Irish former exciseman, of a new still which he patented in 1832; this allowed the distillation of grain whisky to take place in a continuous process in one still. The new process cut back on costs, allowing the Lowland grain distillers to use even less malted barley than before, and to produce on an even bigger scale. Ironically, however, the success of the Excise Act and the new patent still brought trouble for the industry during the mid nineteenth century, because of overproduction and despite the exploiting of new export markets in the Empire and overseas. This development saw the foreshadowing of the emergence of the Distillers Company, with the combining in a price-fixing cartel of the six biggest Lowland grain whisky producers; they were not to join together officially, however, until 1877, by which time the face of the industry had changed dramatically.

This change was brought about by the development of techniques of blending malt and grain whiskies to produce a lighter spirit than the traditional single malt, and a more flavoursome one than grain whisky. In the 1850s Andrew Usher, the Edinburgh whisky merchant who was agent for the

A detail from an 1870 illustration showing the internal workings of the Coffey Still

Glenlivet whiskies, had vatted together several casks of Glenlivet from his stocks, producing in the process a much more consistent product. The practice was soon extended to the blending of malt and grain. This was held to produce a lighter spirit which English drinkers, un-used to the much stronger malt product of the pot still, found much more palatable. It also introduced an element of

Andrew Usher, first chairman of the North British Distillery Co. and a pioneer of blending

consistency to the product. Coincidentally, this development came when reserves of brandy, the first-choice spirit in England, were threatened as a result of the Phylloxera blight in the French vineyards in the 1860s. Timely exploitation of the market in England by the grain producers and blenders meant that, as stocks of brandy declined in the 1870s and '80s, the new blended whiskies came to take their place as the qual-ity spirit, and the 1890s was a period of unprecedented growth for the Scottish whisky industry. New malt distilleries were opened and groups like Distillers and the North British Distillery Company, serving the interests of the grain distillers and the blenders respectively, became phenomenally successful. The whisky industry was developing to become recognizable as the industry it is today.

The boom period was followed, typically, by a slump, and difficult times for the industry at the beginning of this century were compounded by the First World War and the introduction of Prohibition in the USA in 1920. The years from then to the Second World War saw a drop in output of almost 50%, and an almost complete halt being brought to the production of malt whisky. This situation continued after the war when, naturally, what grain was available had to be diverted to feed the people rather than make whisky. As prosperity returned in the 1950s, whisky output increased and exports rose. New distilleries were built in the 1960s, old ones reopened, and the production of malt whisky quadrupled in a decade. Take-over and consolidation were the keynotes of the industry in the 1970s, with English brewers moving into the whisky market on a large scale. This trend culminated in the messy take-over of the Distillers Company (now United Distillers) by Guinness, a transaction which resulted in the chairman of the brewing giant and several of his advisers ending up in court. Ironically, however, the adage of there being no bad publicity seems to be borne out by the Distillers take-over: an episode which apparently brought the industry into disrepute, came at a time when the market was picking up again after the slump lasting from the mid '70s to the mid '80s, and served to give whisky a timely publicity boost.

This upturn in the drink's fortunes continued into the 1990s, with the emphasis in marketing being placed on quality rather than quantity: cheaper blends have tended to

Lochranza Distillery on the Isle of Arran. Opened in 1995, it is Scotland's newest distillery (Isle of Arran Distiller Ltd).

disappear, single malts are taking an increasing share of the market, and price rises are being met by consumers, who seem to prefer the new expensive-and-exclusive image of the drink. Increasing importance was placed on packaging and advertising, and with the marketing of new visitor centres in the distilleries themselves as tourist attractions in their own right. By 1995, however, growth in the Scotch market as a whole had slowed once again and the industry was having to work hard to maintain its position. The premium end of the industry continued to be healthy (helped no doubt by the first reduction in excise duty for a hundred years) although the mass-market sector faced increasing competition, particularly from vodka producers. It responded by the creation of whisky-based drinks designed to appeal to a younger, less traditional customer base – whiskies spiked with red chilli peppers, for example – but by 1998 the producing companies had largely decided to abandon such experiments. Instead, it turned to television advertising in an attempt to woo younger consumers in both the UK and the USA. The full impact of such TV advertising may not be seen for several years.

One the biggest challenges facing the drinks industry in recent years was the abandonment of duty-free facilities within the European Union in 1999; this was a potentially harsh blow to the Scotch producers to whom the duty-free market is worth some £80 million. Nevertheless, after experiencing difficult trading conditions in 1997 and 1998 (particularly for export sales to the Far East and the USA), the industry looks set to begin the new century with a renewed confidence and buoyancy with the prospect of important new markets opening up in China and India, and with the continuing growth in the sales of single malts.

How Scotch Whisky is Made

*T*wo different processes are used for the distillation of Scotch malt and grain whiskies.

Malt whisky

In malt whisky distillation, there are several basic steps to the process: malting, mashing, fermentation, distillation and maturation, although the minor elements may vary from one distillery to another. Barley may be bought in pre-malted, but if it is not, it is first filtered to remove any foreign matter.

(1) **Malting**. The process begins when the barley is transferred to soak in tanks of water which go by the self-explanatory name of barley steeps; this process takes two to four days. In the traditional process, the barley is then spread on a malting floor, to be turned by hand daily for the next twelve days or so, allowing it to sprout; now, however, most distilleries use mechanical devices for turning the sprouting barley. As the seeds germinate, the starch in the barley releases some of its sugars. At the appropriate moment, germination is stopped by drying the cereal in a malt kiln over a peat furnace or fire. The peat smoke which flavours the drying barley at this stage can, depending on its intensity, be tasted in the final whisky itself. The malt kilns traditionally had the pagoda-style roofs which were such an instantly recognizable characteristic of the malt distilleries; these can still be seen on older distilleries.

(2) **Mashing**. The next stage for the malted barley is passage

Turning the barley by hand on a traditional malting floor (Scotch Whisky Association)

through a mill, from which it emerges roughly ground as grist. From here it is moved to a mash tun, a large vat where it is mixed with hot water and agitated, so that its sugars dissolve to produce wort, a sweet, non-alcoholic liquid. This process is repeated to ensure that all the sugars have been collected. The solid remains of the barley are removed at this point for conversion to cattle food.

(3) **Fermentation**. The wort is cooled and transferred to washbacks, large vats where yeast is added and the process of fermentation begins. The chemical reaction which takes place with the addition of the yeast converts the sugars in the wort to alcohol, a process which takes around two days and results in a low-strength alcoholic liquid now called wash.

A traditional pagoda-topped malting kiln (Scotch Whisky Association)

Washbacks where the wort is fermented to produce the wash (Scotch Whisky Association)

How Scotch malt whisky is made

Malt Kiln

Ma
Bi

Barley
Steep

Malt

Malting Floor

Peat
Furnace

1. Malting

Condenser

Condenser

Wash Still

Spirit
Still

S

Furnace

Furnace

4. Distillation

Mashing Water Tank

Grist Hopper

Mashing Machine

Mash Tun

Mashing

Washback

3. Fermentation

Warehouse Vat

Casks

5. Maturation

(4) **Distillation.** The wash is then ready for the stills. The shape of the still is one of the most important factors in the whisky-making process, as it can have a decisive influence on the final character of the malt whisky: for instance, a still with a short neck will produce a whisky with heavier oils and a more intense flavour, whereas lighter-flavoured whiskies with less heavy oils will emerge from a still with a long or high neck. The first still which the wash passes through is known, appropriately, as the wash still, and here it is heated.

As the alcohol has a lower boiling point than water, the alcoholic steam rises up the still through its long spout to the worm, a condensing coil. The distillate, now called low wines, is passed into the second still, the spirit still, where the process is repeated, with the liquid running off into the glass-fronted spirit safe.

It is at this point that the skill of the distiller is crucial: unable to smell or taste the liquid to judge it, he must know when to separate the middle cut, or main run

Copper wash stills (Scotch Whisky Association)

Drawing a sample of new whisky from the spirit sample safe (Glenturret Distillery Ltd)

of the spirit, which contains the best-quality alcohol needed for malt whisky, from the foreshots (the raw, poisonous first distillate) and the feints, or aftershots, which contain a lower grade of alcohol. Once separated, foreshots and feints are fed back into the wash for redistillation.

(5) **Maturation**. The main run of the alcohol is now transferred for storage to a vat and is mixed with water to bring it down in strength. It is then transferred into casks for maturing. The whole process of distillation can theoretically be completed inside a week, but the whisky must now mature for at least three years before it can be sold; during this time, a small percentage of the whisky, known as the 'angels' share', will evaporate. In practice, malt whiskies are left to mature for an average of eight to fifteen years.

Maturing casks (Glenturret Distillery Ltd)

Grain whisky

With the exception of the Invergordon Distillery, all grain distilleries are located in the Lowlands. Grain distilleries use patent (or Coffey) stills, which can operate continuously. The basic process used is similar to that for malt, up to the point of distillation, although everything takes place on a much larger scale, and with much less malted barley: maize, unmalted barley or other cereals are generally used.

Distillation is carried out in two large cylindrical columns which are linked by pipes. The wash passes into the first column, the rectifier, in a coiled pipe running through its length. Jets of steam are forced up into the column, through a series of perforated plates between which the coiled pipe passes, heating the wash inside before it passes out and into the analyser. In the analyser the wash is no longer in the coiled pipe, and it is now met by another jet of steam passing through more perforated plates. The steam and evaporated alcohol rise and are passed back into the rectifier, with the alcohol cooling as it moves up, encountering fresh, cold wash in the coiled pipe on its way down, until it reaches a cold water coil where it condenses before passing out of the still. The impure alcohols in the first and last part of the distillate can be redistilled, while the alcohol which reaches the spirit safe and receiver is very pure. The whisky will mature faster than malt, and is less subject to variable factors. The vast majority of the produce will go for blending not long after its three-year maturation period has passed.

Blending

*B*lending is a slightly separate part of the whisky-making process, with a third product being made from malt and grain whiskies. It both guarantees consistency of the brand and aims to create a new whisky of character in its own right. It is a process which absorbs the greater part of the distilleries' production, and is the mainstay of the industry.

The process was developed on a commercial footing in the second half of the nineteenth century. Although it may initially have been used as a way of stretching further supplies of the more expensive malt whisky, it was the means by which whisky was popularized first in the English market, then overseas.

The blender at work (Scotch Whisky Association and overleaf)

Blending is an olfactory craft, with blenders nosing rather than tasting whiskies. It is a highly skilled profession, with anything from 20 to 50 different whiskies being mixed in any one brand, including varieties of type, region, distillery and age. The new whisky's character is dependent on how well these different component whiskies complement and contrast with one another to bring out their various flavours. The high number of component whiskies is the blender's guarantee of consistency: if one contributing distillery goes out of production, the consistency of the blend can be maintained more easily than if there were a lesser number of whiskies, each with a stronger presence, as ingredients.

The ingredients and their proportions are closely guarded secrets, although it is generally assumed that where a blender owns a distillery, the distillery's produce will be represented to some degree in the blend: so, for example, the produce of Laphroaig Distillery, which is owned by Allied Distillers, is present in their Long John, Ballantine's and Teacher's blends. The produce of some distilleries is never bottled as a single malt, and goes entirely for blending.

After the whiskies are matured, they are mixed together in their correct proportions in a vat, then 'married' in oak casks for at least a year to allow intermingling and further maturation to take place. As with most malts, the blend is reduced to the correct strength by the addition of water. Burnt-sugar caramel may be added to bring a blend up to its desired colour before the whisky is filtered, bottled and labelled.

Different Types of Scotch Whisky

*T*here are particular legal constraints on what can be termed Scotch whisky, the most basic of which dictate the components of the whisky (cereals, malt and yeast), the maximum alcoholic strength at distillation (94.8% alcohol by volume), and the minimum length of maturation (at least three years). Finally, the whisky itself must have been distilled and matured in Scotland.

Scotland produces two main types of whisky, and all the available varieties of the spirit are variations on these themes. The first is malt whisky, made from malted barley, using a pot still; and the second is grain whisky, made from other cereals – maize or unmalted barley, together with a little malted barley – in a patent still. The two types' distillation processes are explained on pp. 19–27; what follows here is an explanation of the varieties in which they are available.

Single malt is the product of one distillery. Legally, it can be sold after only three years' maturation, but in practice it is generally left to mature from between eight to fifteen years, by which time its character and flavour has become more pronounced and rounded. Generally, whiskies of varying proof strengths and ages from different casks are mixed together, ensuring a consistent distillery product (as the product of any one distillation will inevitably not be identical to any other), although the age which appears on the label is always the age of the youngest distillation in the bottle. Malts are diluted from their cask strength (up to mid 60s percentage alcohol by volume) to 40% or 43% for commercial marketing. Single malts comprise a relatively small, although increasing, proportion of the total whisky market.

A sub-group of single malt whisky is the **single-cask malt**. Generally available commercially only through specialist shops and independent merchants (see pp. 49–51), these are whiskies which, as the name suggests, are the produce of one distillation, bottled straight from the cask and not vatted with any other produce from the distillery. This process, together with the absence of chill filtration before the whiskies are bottled, ensures that the particular character of a distillery's whisky – and, indeed, of a specific distillation – is unmasked, and greatly emphasized. Supplies of a particular variety or distillation are, by nature, finite. This is the most expensive type of whisky, often costing at least double the price of a normal, distillery-bottled single malt, but felt by many whisky drinkers to be well worth the expense.

A **vatted malt** is the final of the malt whisky sub-groups. This type of whisky has a long pedigree, having formed the basis of the first blended whisky in the mid nineteenth century. Vatted malts are normally produced by blenders and big companies who have a variety of malt distilleries from which to take their product. It could be regarded as a half-way house between a blend and a single malt, although the flavours in some vatted malts can be just as well developed as those in a single. Single malts of different distilleries and different ages are mixed together, the age (if any) on the label being that of the youngest whisky in the mixture. The words 'vatted malt' normally do not appear on a label; instead, the absence of the word 'single' before 'malt', together with an absence of a distillery name, is generally an indicator of a vatted malt.

Grain whisky has been mentioned briefly above, and in proportion to the quantities in which it is produced, very little of it is bottled in its own right. Instead, its main function is as a component part of a blend.

Blended whiskies are a mixture of malt and grain, not necessarily in any fixed proportions but rather in a recipe which will achieve the blender's desired balance in terms of character, cost and quality. Blends were the means in the nineteenth century by which hitherto too-strongly flavoured malt whiskies were mellowed for the palate in markets outside Scotland – firstly for England, then for export markets. The desired aim of a blender is not to dilute or diminish the flavours of the various component whiskies, but rather to choose ones which are both compatible and complementary, resulting in the creation of a new whisky of distinctive character. In this way, consistency of the product can also be assured. Blended whiskies, of which there are over a thousand, comprise the greater part of the whisky market. The major blenders generally own both malt and grain distilleries, so it is safe to assume that the product of a particular malt distillery will be represented to some degree in its owner's blends.

A **de luxe whisky** is a particular type of blend, recognized to be of superior quality to a standard blend. De luxe whiskies generally contain a higher proportion of malt which is older, more mature and consequently more expensive. Some de luxes carry an age statement on their label; as with other whiskies, this is the age of the youngest component in the bottle.

Blends, but of a quite different type, is a name which can be given to the growing market for whisky **liqueurs**. Some of these contain whisky flavoured with honey, fruits, herbs and spices, while the cream liqueurs also contain whisky, but are more inclined towards cream, coffee and chocolate in their flavours.

Regional Characteristics of Scotch Malt Whisky

*T*he qualities and characteristics associated with particular producing regions are not a result of current tastes and fashions, but rather a legacy of the past. In times when roads were often poor or, at some times of the year, non-existent, when communications were often difficult, sometimes dangerous and always time-consuming, and trade between different parts of the country was expensive, it was obvious that a distillery would use the raw materials and ingredients which were to hand in a particular locality rather than go to the trouble of importing produce from other areas. These factors, combined with local climate and geology, helped produce whiskies which varied in character from one part of the country to another.

The current chief distinction, between Highland and Lowland whiskies, is also a legacy of a past legal and fiscal policy. As a means of controlling the trade and movement of whisky from the Highlands to the Lowlands (whose cheaper, coarser grain spirit was then successfully being exported into England), the Highland dividing line was established, following roughly the Highland Boundary Fault Line, which runs from the Firth of Clyde to the Firth of Tay. The distinction remained, even with the equalizing of quality between malts from north and south of the line, and is still recognized today. The maps on pp. 38–39 and 42–43 show all existing distilleries within the broad categorizations that follow.

Lowland malts are defined as those coming from the southern half of Scotland – that is, from south of the Highland line. In terms of their taste, the Lowland malts are perhaps a good first stepping stone into the wider world of malt whiskies for the drinker who wants to graduate from blends: relatively unassertive in character, they are generally soft and light, with a gentle sweetness which ensures them many fans among more experienced palates. Much of the produce of the Lowland malt distilleries is used in blends.

As a once-popular music-hall ditty more colourfully suggested, **Campbeltown** was a major centre of whisky production. Over twenty distilleries operated there in the later nineteenth century, encouraged by the abundance of local supplies of peat, barley from the Mull of Kintyre, and a nearby source of cheap coal. However, over-production, too-wide variations in quality and the exhaustion of the local coal seam contributed to the decline of the local industry, to the point where only two distilleries now remain. With the shift in emphasis from sea-borne to road traffic, it is unlikely that the town will ever again regain its former eminence. Nevertheless, it still retains its regional classification. Campbeltown whiskies are generally accepted to be quite distinctive, with a character which is mellower than that of the Islay malts, with a smoothness and a variable peatiness in the flavour.

Islay malts must be, for everyone from the beginner to the connoisseur, the most distinctive of all single malt whiskies – certainly, their flavour is among the strongest of all the regions. Peat is the key, both in terms of its influence on the

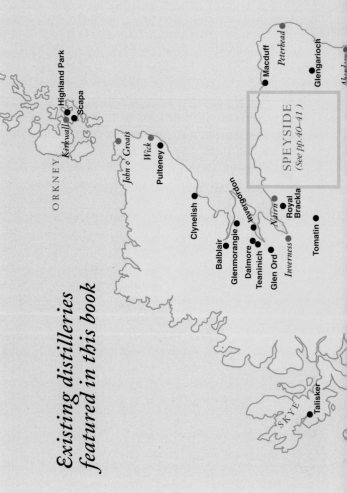

Existing distilleries
featured in this book

ingredients used for distillation and of its presence in the final taste. The island has extensive beds of peat, over which the water used in the distillation process flows, arriving at its destination already flavoured. Varying amounts of peat are also used to dry the barley. In the past this latter ingredient, too, was produced locally, although now it may be brought in. Peat is noticeable in the flavours of all the Islay malts, from the mildest to the most intensely flavoured, imparting a dryness which is sometimes balanced by sweetness, sometimes emphasized by smokiness. For beginners to single malts, the Islay whiskies seem like an acquired taste, but they are an essential ingredient in the whisky-blending process, and the chances are that what you may think of as the distinctively Scottish flavour in your whisky is imparted by their presence in a blend.

Finally, the largest region, with more distilleries than the rest of the country combined, is **Highland,** probably the quintessential Scottish whisky production area. This is the land which lies to the north of the Highland line and includes distilleries as far apart as Inchmurrin in Dunbartonshire, Oban in Argyll, Pulteney in Wick and Highland Park in Orkney. As might be expected across such a wide area, generalizations become less valid and sub-division becomes more necessary. Geographical divisions of north, south, east and west, together with a special one for Speyside, can be useful in illustrating particular characteristics.

The north Highland malts can be said to stretch from the area around Inverness up the east coast to Wick. The whiskies from this area are generally smooth, and while ranging from dry to fruity sweet, are not normally quite as peaty as some of their more southerly neighbours. Whisky from the southern Highlands – generally speaking, around the Perthshire area and to the west – is, as might be expected, softer and lighter in character, often reasonably sweet but with one or two dry examples. The western Highlands is the smallest of the Highland sub-divisions, encompassing the area from Oban to Fort William with their smooth, rounded whiskies.

The eastern Highlands has distilleries spread out along the North Sea coast from Brechin in the south to Banff in the north. The whiskies in this area offer a wide range of styles, one of the widest of any of the sub-divisions, from fruity sweetness to peaty dryness.

The largest and most famous of the Highland sub-divisions is that of **Speyside**, producing a range of single malts whose names are instantly recognizable, even to non-whisky drinkers: Macallan, Glenfiddich, Glenfarclas and Glenlivet. The area is concentrated around the Elgin–Dufftown district, a picturesque and fertile area whose remoteness made it an

Inchgower   Glenglassaugh

Buckie

Spey

Aultmore   Knockdhu

Strathisla   Deveron

Grant   Auchroisk

Glentauchers   Glen Keith   *Keith*

Macallan

Craigellachie

Convalmore   *Huntly*

lvenie   Glenfiddich

ftown   Glendullan

ufftown   Mortlach

Glendronach

Fiddich

Ardmore

Existing Speyside distilleries featured in this book

ideal location for the whisky smugglers of past centuries to escape the efforts of the excisemen. Speyside whiskies are recognized as being mellow, with a malty sweetness and light notes of peat: beyond this basic generalization, however, lies a wealth of variety and subtlety, and the Speyside malts can range from the aromatic and flowery to the robust and sherried. Whiskies can be found in this area to satisfy all palates, from the novice to the connoisseur, and for all occasions.

The final Highland sub-group is that of the **Island** whiskies. As might be expected when these are viewed on a map, the classification is not so much based on characteristics as convenience – this is a suitable sub-group in which to deal with the remaining whiskies which do not fit in any other.

At present, the islands concerned are Jura, Mull and Skye in the west, and Orkney in the north. (It does not, of course, include Islay, whose distinctive style merits a category of its own.) However, in 1995 the Isle of Arran was added to this list with the opening of the first legal distillery on the island for 160 years at Lochranza. (The single malt produced here was not due to be available early in the new century but the distillery's microclimate allowed the whisky to mature at a faster rate than originally expected and the first bottles of Arran Single Malt were launched in 1999.) Once again, generalizations are difficult to make, with characters ranging from reasonably dry to full, sweet and malty.

As with any classification, these listings should not be taken as hard and fast rules – taste and preferences vary so greatly that they can only be general guidelines. The best way to decide how well particular whiskies fit their supposed regional listing or characteristic is simply to try each one for yourself!

Visiting Scotch Distilleries and Producers

*W*ith more than 250,000 people visiting Scotland's distilleries every year, catering for visitors has become an important means of promotion and source of revenue for the more famous whisky-makers. Many distilleries are happy to accept visitors, and facilities range from a friendly, impromptu guided tour to a high-tech reception centre with organized tour and gift shop.

Once you have decided which distilleries you would like to visit, you can telephone in advance to find out the particular facilities they offer – the telephone numbers of those distilleries which are equipped to receive visitors are given under their entries throughout the book. It is particularly advisable to telephone if you plan to visit during July and August. Although this is the height of the tourist season, it is also the traditional 'silent' period for this industry which was so closely associated with farming: closing the distillery at this time meant that the workers could help to gather in the harvest. The Scotch Whisky Association (tel: [Edinburgh] 0131-222 9200; [London] 0171-629 4384) publishes a useful leaflet detailing over forty distilleries which welcome visitors, together with opening times and booking information. The Scotch Whisky Heritage Centre (tel: 0131-220 0441) and the Scottish Tourist Board (head office, tel: 0131-332 2433) are also useful sources of information.

If you are in Edinburgh, a visit to the Scotch Whisky

The Pagoda Room Restaurant, part of the award-winning Glenturret Visitor Centre at Crieff in Perthshire (Glenturret Distillery Ltd)

Heritage Centre on Castlehill is always a good starting point if you want to find out more about the industry, with exhibits which are both fun and educational. You can travel back through the industry's past, including the days of illicit distillation, viewing all from the comfort of your own motorized whisky cask!

Finally, for the opportunity to see a perfectly preserved traditional distillery, Dallas Dhu at Forres should not be missed if you are travelling through the north east. Established at the end of the nineteenth century, it stands in lovely countryside to the south of the town. It was previously owned by the Distillers Company, who closed it in 1983, and is now operated by the Historic Scotland. Although it no longer produces whisky, it offers one of the most interesting distillery visits in Scotland (telephone: 01309-676548 for opening times).

Towser, the late distillery mouse catcher at Glenturret Distillery. In a career spanning 24 years, Towser caught 28,899 mice, a feat which earned her an entry in the Guinness Book of Records. *She died in 1987 and was succeeded by a new distillery cat, Amber (Glenturret Distillery Ltd)*

Professional Bodies, Merchants and Trade Associations

*A*s explained on pp. 32–33, single malts bottled by the distilleries are generally a marrying of casks from several distillations, with water being added to reduce the whisky to an agreed alcohol by volume strength for bottling. The whisky will also generally undergo a process of cold-temperature filtration to remove the residues which naturally precipitate cloudiness in the drink after dilution, when it is kept at low temperatures, or when it has ice added. Views differ as to whether this alters the character and taste of the whisky: the producers cite scientific evidence to show that there is no alteration to the whisky's character if it is not diluted below 40% alcohol by volume. However, various independent bodies believe that it does, and they offer consumers the chance to test for themselves.

The Scotch Malt Whisky Society (tel: 0131-554 3451) is one of these bodies. It buys from the distilleries selected single malts which it bottles straight from the cask and offers to its members, of whom there are over 18,000 around the world. The society aims to promote the increased understanding, appreciation and discerning consumption of malt whisky and has recently begun day-long whisky schools comprising practicals, lectures and tastings.

The independent spirit merchants, William Cadenhead Ltd (tel: 01586-554258), also subscribe to this view of the chill-filtration process, and pride themselves on maintaining the individuality of each batch of whisky, bottling straight from the cask at cask strength. The company's approach, of minimal interference with the whisky, relatively simple packaging, and the taking of care over content rather than presentation, is designed to appeal to the slightly more experienced whisky drinker. Much of Cadenhead's stock comes from distilleries whose produce is not otherwise available to the public.

The distinctive labels of independent bottlers, William Cadenhead (left) and Gordon and MacPhail (right)

Gordon and MacPhail of Elgin (tel: 01343-545111) also offer a wide range of their own bottlings from many distilleries. The company, owned and run by the Urquhart family, was established in 1895 as a wine and spirit merchant and licensed grocers, and now is regarded as the world's leading malt whisky specialists. Gordon and MacPhail's policy has always been to buy new whisky direct from a distillery, often in their own casks, warehousing it themselves and bottling it when they consider it to be at its best. Each barrel is assessed for quality, style and quantity available prior to bottling, thereby achieving a consistency and quality of malt for which the company is recognized. As well as single and vatted malts, cask-strength bottlings and unusual blends, they have a large selection of old and rare whiskies.

A relative newcomer to the independent merchants' ranks is the Signatory Vintage Scotch Whisky Company, based in Edinburgh (tel: 0131-555 4988). Founded in the late 1980s, they acquire casks of exceptional age and quality and bottle either diluted to 40%, 43% or 46%, or at cask strength. No colourant is used in their bottlings and only the diluted range is chill-filtered to remove oiliness. There is a variation between bottlings as the number of casks vatted varies.

For those whose interest is in the packaging as much as the contents, the Mini Bottle Club is the world's premier club for collectors of miniatures. Details can be obtained from the membership secretary, c/o 47 Burradon Rd, Burradon, Northumberland NE23 7NF (enclose a s.a.e.).

Finally, if you would like to know more about any aspect of Scotch whisky, the Scotch Whisky Association will happily supply information for you. The association promotes the interests of the Scotch whisky industry in Britain and around the world, and its membership comprises almost all companies involved in the industry. The Public Affairs office is in London (tel: 0171-629 4384), while the head office is in Edinburgh (tel: 0131-222 9200).

Reading the Label

*T*he label on a whisky bottle will allow you to identify a few basic facts about its contents even before you open the bottle – most obviously, the brand and its producers, the type of whisky it is, and its age, quantity and strength. Single malts normally proclaim themselves as such, and the identification of the producing distillery acts as a double check. A label which states a bottle's contents to be malt, but without the words 'single' or 'unblended', is probably vatted. Grains and blends likewise will identify themselves, and while most de luxe whiskies will also do so, this is not always the case. Blends of all kinds will carry the name of the blenders rather than of any distillery.

Where whiskies carry an age statement on the label, this will be the age of the youngest whisky in the bottle. Instead of this, some malts may give the year of their distillation. Single malts are usually eight years old and upwards, becoming more expensive as their age increases. It is generally held, however, that up to fifteen years is a good maturation period for whisky, and while some whiskies improve by maturing beyond this period, not all do of necessity – it depends on the individual whisky. Whiskies for general consumption in the UK are normally packaged in 70 or 75 cl bottles, but you may also come upon 1 litre bottles.

Most whiskies are sold at 40% alcohol by volume. The system for measuring spirit strength in Britain changed in

brand name

type of whisky

age of whisky

distiller

strength (alcohol by volume))

bottle volume

VATTED MALT

BLEND

DE LUXE

The component parts of a single malt whisky label (top), together with examples of labels from other types of whisky

1980 from the older and more complicated Sikes system of measuring proof strength, to the Organization of Legal Metrology, or OIML system, which measures spirit strength as a percentage of volume at 20 °C. Whisky is distilled at a much higher content than its final form for consumption. Water may be added before it goes into the cask, to bring it down to 68.5% alcohol by volume, a standard measure. Some evaporation takes place as the whisky matures, leaving a final cask strength of around 45–60%. Cask-strength whiskies are available, but most single malts have to have water added to bring them down to 40% or 43% (normally for the export market) strength for bottling. However, the industry may move towards a standard strength of 40% after a 1988 European Community directive which based the amount of duty on the alcoholic strength of a spirit. 40% alcohol by volume is equivalent to the old measure of 70° proof and, confusingly, 80° proof in the USA, which uses a slightly different system again.

The
Whiskies
of
Scotland

Taste Rating

*T*he discussions on the different whiskies which follow contain a taste rating of 1–5. This is not intended to be a judgement on the quality or relative standard of the spirit, nor is it possible to place strength and flavour together satisfactorily. Rather, it can be used as an indicator of accessibility of the whisky for a relatively inexperienced palate. A whisky may be mild or strong and still either lack flavour or exude it, so this rating concerns the degree of flavour, while at the same time allowing for the strength interfering with a person's ability to appreciate the flavour. The basic categories are as follows:

1   Popular with particular palates; spirituous, with a very mild flavour

2   Good for beginners; appealing taste and flavour for most palates at certain times

2–3 Also good for beginners, but a little stronger than **2**. One to return to again and again

3   A dram for everyone; not too powerful, with pleasant sensations

3–4 This should also appeal to most tastes, but is slightly stronger, so the palate requires a little more experience

4   Very pleasing; a stronger spirit, ideal for those with more experience

5   Robust; only for the well developed palate

HIGHLAND
SINGLE MALT
SCOTCH WHISKY

ABERFELDY

distillery was established in
1898 on the *road* to *Perth* and
south *side* of the *RIVER TAY*.
Fresh *spring water* is taken
from the *nearby PITILIE*
burn and used to produce this
UNIQUE single MALT
SCOTCH WHISKY with its
distinctive PEATY *nose*.

AGED 15 YEARS

Distilled & Bottled in SCOTLAND
ABERFELDY DISTILLERY
Aberfeldy, Perthshire, Scotland

43% vol 70 cl

Aberfeldy

Aberfeldy Distillery,
Aberfeldy, Perthshire

TYPE

Single malt

BOTTLING AGE

15 years

STRENGTH

43%

TASTE RATING

3

MINIATURES

Yes

COMMENTS

Basically a dry malt with a
medium body and clean, fresh
character, but with a distinctly
peaty background.

VISITORS

Visitors are welcome 0930–1630
Mon.–Fri. (times are restricted
in winter). Telephone 01887-
820330.

*A*berfeldy Distillery stands
near the River Tay, at the
town from which it takes its name.
Building began in 1896 and the
distillery opened two years later. It
was built by Dewar but passed with
that company into the ownership of
the Distillers Company Ltd in 1925. It
is now by John Dewar & Sons and
much of its production goes into
blends such as Dewar's White Label.
The single malt is still relatively rare,
only becoming available in official
bottlings in the Distillery (Flora and
Fauna) Malts series early in the 1990s.

Aberlour

Aberlour-Glenlivet Distillery,
Aberlour, Banffshire

TYPE
Single malt

BOTTLING AGE
10, 12, 15, 18, 21 years

STRENGTH
40%, 43%, Cask strength

TASTE RATING
3

MINIATURES
Yes

COMMENTS
A smooth, rich, sherried Speyside malt which is an ideal after-dinner drink.

VISITORS
Visitors are welcome but only by appointment. Telephone 01340-871204 to arrange.

*E*stablished in the 1860s, Aberlour Distillery was rebuilt in the early 1880s after its destruction in a fire. It sits below Ben Rinnes from whose slopes it draws its water, said to be an important characteristic of its distinctive flavour. In the distillery grounds is the well of St Drostan (or Dunstan), the tenth-century missionary and patron saint of Aberlour who later became Archbishop of Canterbury. Since its acquisition by the Pernod Ricard company in 1974, Aberlour has been well marketed in France, where it is one of the most popular of Scotch whiskies. The company also owns the Irish Distillers Group.

An Cnoc

*Knockdhu Distillery,
Knock, Banffshire*

TYPE	
Single malt	
BOTTLING AGE	
12 years	
STRENGTH	
40%	
TASTE RATING	
2–3	
MINIATURES	
Yes	

COMMENTS

An Cnoc's dryish aroma is complemented by a mellow sweetness in the flavour. This Highland malt was previously known as Knockdhu.

VISITORS

The distillery is not open to visitors.

*K*nockdhu Distillery was established in 1893 on a favoured site: with water available from Knock Hill, barley from the nearby farmlands, and a good supply of local peat. Although both its buildings and machinery have since been modified, the production process remains essentially the same, with the two originally designed pot stills remaining. Previously owned by Distillers Company Ltd and licensed to Haig, Knockdhu was sold in 1988 to Inver House Distillers, who reopened it after a lengthy silent period. Its single malt is one of the few which does not take its distillery's name.

The Antiquary

J. & W. Hardie, Glasgow

TYPE
De luxe blend

BOTTLING AGE
12, 21 years

STRENGTH
40%, 43%

TASTE RATING
3

MINIATURES
Yes

COMMENTS
A smooth, well-balanced, premium blend which displays the mellowness expected from its blend of whiskies all aged 12 years and over.

*T*he Antiquary takes its name from the novel by Sir Walter Scott and was the creation of John and William Hardie, who founded their partnership in Edinburgh in 1857. The brand was first introduced into the market in 1888. In February 1996, the Tomatin Distillery Company purchased The Antiquary from United Distillers and it is now marketed by J. & W. Hardie, a wholly owned subsidiary of Tomatin. As well as a loyal following at home, The Antiquary sells particularly well in Spain, France and Italy, and a 21-year-old bottling was introduced in 1999 to further expand the brand.

Ardbeg

Ardbeg Distillery,
Port Ellen, Islay, Argyll

TYPE

Single malt

BOTTLING AGE

Varies

STRENGTH

17 years, 1978 vintage

TASTE RATING

5

MINIATURES

Yes

COMMENTS

With a dominant peaty aroma and salty, orangey overtones, Ardbeg's insistently smoky flavour is balanced by sweeter notes. Ardbeg is considered to be one of the finest Islay malts.

VISITORS

Visitors are welcome: 1000–1600, Mon.–Fri. all year; 1000–1700, Jun.–Aug.; or by appointment. Telephone 01496-302244.

*T*his distillery was opened in 1815, and was one of several established near the sea in an area which was originally used by smugglers. It was bought by Hiram Walker in the 1950s, primarily to use its produce in blending. Nearby Lochs Uigeadale and Arinambeast supply the water which, together with local peat, produces a distinctively Islay malt. While under Allied Distillers' ownership, the single malt was not officially produced (and was only available from independent bottllers). After its purchase in 1997 by Glenmorangie plc, the distillery was restored and the single malt relaunched as a distillery bottling.

Ardmore

*Ardmore Distillery,
Kennethmont, Aberdeenshire*

TYPE

Single malt

BOTTLING AGE

Varies

STRENGTH

Varies

TASTE RATING

4

MINIATURES

Yes

COMMENTS

A full-bodied Speyside malt which is both robust and sweet. An ideal after-dinner dram, though not easy to come by; available as a single malt only through independent bottlers.

VISITORS

Visitors are welcome by appointment. Telephone 01464-3213 to arrange.

*T*he distillery at Ardmore was built in 1898 by the Teacher family of whisky merchants and blenders. Since that time almost all its production has gone into Teacher's blends, most famously Highland Cream. Today it is operated by Allied Distillers, so its product also features prominently in Allied's other blends. Although the distillery has been modernized it still retains some of the original equipment, such as coal-fired stills, which were used in the production of whisky at the end of the nineteenth century.

A unique *Single Island* Malt Scotch *Whisky*

Arran

Captures the *Character* of this *Beautiful* Island of *Clear Mountain* water & soft *Sea Air.*

70 cl   *Matured in Sherry Casks*   43%vol.

Arran

Isle of Arran Distillers,
Lochranza, Isle of Arran

TYPE
Single malt

STRENGTH
43%

TASTE RATING
3

MINIATURES
Yes

COMMENTS
Scotland's newest and freshest malt, Arran has a gentle peaty aroma with tangerine overtones that are also evident in the finish.

VISITORS
The distillery and visitor centre are open daily, Mar.–Oct.

S ituated on the north of the island at Lochranza, Scotland's newest malt whisky distillery went into production in 1994. One of the few independent distillers in the industry, the company has invested in traditional methods of production within a state-of-the-art building. Having laid the first of a new spirit down in 1995 in special sherry casks, the company was surprised to find that a selection of it matured more rapidly than anticipated, possibly due to the island's warm microclimate. In 1999, it launched this limited edition of the single malt, the first produced on the island for over 150 years.

Auchentoshan

*Auchentoshan Distillery,
Dalmuir, Dunbartonshire*

TYPE

Single malt

BOTTLING AGE

Not specified, 10, 21, 22,
25, 31 years

STRENGTH

40%, 43%

TASTE RATING

2–3

MINIATURES

Yes

COMMENTS

A light, sweetish whisky whose smooth qualities are perhaps partially owed to the process of triple, rather than the more common double distillation.

VISITORS

The distillery is not open to visitors.

*A*lthough Auchentoshan Distillery lies south of the Highland Line (the line initiated by the Customs and Excise to differentiate area boundaries between styles of whisky), it uses water from north of the line, so theoretically could be said to have a foot in both camps. But it is officially recognized as a Lowland distillery and whisky. Founded in 1823, part of its interesting history includes surviving bombing in the Clydebank Blitz during the Second World War, when a stream of blazing whisky was said to have flowed from the building. It is presently owned by Morrison Bowmore Distillers Ltd, also owners of Bowmore and Glen Garioch distilleries.

SPEYSIDE
SINGLE MALT *SCOTCH WHISKY*

AULTMORE

distillery located between *KEITH* and *BUCKIE* began production in 1897. The name, derived from the *Gaelic*, means "*big burn*". Ideal supplies of *water* and *peat* from the *Foggie Moss* made this area a haunt of *illicit distillers* in the past. Water from the *Barn of AUCHINDERRAN* is now used to produce this *smooth, well balanced single MALT 1/2 SCOTCH WHISKY* with a *mellow* finish.

AGED **12** YEARS

43% VOL Distilled & Bottled in *SCOTLAND.* AULTMORE DISTILLERY Keith, Banffshire, Scotland. **70 cl**

Aultmore

*Aultmore Distillery,
Aultmore, Keith, Banffshire*

TYPE

Single malt

BOTTLING AGE

12 years

STRENGTH

43%

TASTE RATING

3

MINIATURES

Yes

COMMENTS

A faintly peaty aroma leads into this smooth, fruity, well-balanced whisky which has become – deservedly – better known in recent years.

VISITORS

The distillery is open to visitors by appointment only. Telephone 01542-882762.

*A*ultmore Distillery was established in 1895 at the tail-end of the whisky boom by the owner of the older Benrinnes Distillery. The area, with its abundant peat and water supplies, was infamous in the past for illicit distilling. Peat used in the production process is taken from a nearby moss, and the water is taken from local springs. The distillery passed to Dewars in 1923, and was improved and upgraded in the 1970s. It was then owned by United Distillers who bottled a single malt in their Distillery (Flora and Fauna) Malts series. It is now back in the control of John Dewar and Sons.

The Bailie Nicol Jarvie

*MacDonald and Muir,
Leith, Edinburgh*

TYPE

Blend

BOTTLING AGE

No age given

STRENGTH

40%

TASTE RATING

2

MINIATURES

Yes

COMMENTS

A light, subtle whisky with a sweet, well-balanced aroma and a smooth, lingering finish.

*F*ounded in 1893 in Leith by Roderick Macdonald and Alexander Muir, Macdonald and Muir Ltd is one of the few remaining independent family-owned and -controlled companies left in the Scotch whisky trade. 'The Bailie', or 'BNJ' as it is also known, is named after the fictional magistrate in Walter Scott's *Rob Roy*. Although a popular brand in the early years of this century (particularly in military circles), in recent years production had been severely limited. However, the brand was relaunched in October 1994 and production stepped up following a change in the blend receipe.

Balblair

*Balblair Distillery,
Edderton, Tain, Ross-shire*

TYPE

Single malt

BOTTLING AGE

10 years

STRENGTH

40%

TASTE RATING

3

MINIATURES

Yes

COMMENTS

A distinctive Highland malt whose slightly dry sharpness is balanced by a light note of sweetness. Good as an aperitif.

VISITORS

The distillery is not open to visitors.

*A*lthough its origins are lost in the mists of illicit distillation, it is claimed that Balblair was founded in 1749, which would make it one of the oldest distilleries in the country. The present buildings, dating from the 1870s, are set in pretty countryside in an area known as the 'parish of peats'. The distillery had very recently been mothballed by its then owners, Allied Distillers, but was acquired from them in the spring of 1996 by the independent Inver House Distillers. The addition of Balblair gives Inver House five malt distilleries – Balmenach, Knockdhu, Speyburn-Glenlivet and Pulteney, the latter also a recent purchase from Allied.

Ballantine's Finest

Allied Distillers,
Dumbarton, Dunbartonshire

TYPE

Blend

BOTTLING AGE

40%, 43%

STRENGTH

2–3

MINIATURES

Yes

COMMENTS

Ballantine's Finest is, like Allied Distillers' other blends, characteristically mellow and well-rounded with a soft, un-assertive peaty flavour. Their range of blends also includes Ballantine's Gold Seal (12 years old), Ballantine's 17 Years Old and Ballantine's 30-year-old, considered to be one of the oldest (and also one of the most expensive) blends available.

VISITORS

Visitors are welcome by appointment.

*B*allantine's was bought in 1936 by Hiram Walker as one of their first moves into the Scotch whisky market. Glenburgie and Miltonduff distilleries followed in 1937 and their new, giant complex in Dumbarton, featuring grain and malt distilleries, was operational the following year. Today the group is owned by Allied Domecq and operated by their wholly Scottish-based subsidiary, Allied Distillers. The Dumbarton plant is renowned locally for its 'Scotchwatch' alarm system, comprising 100-odd noisy Chinese geese!

Balmenach

*BalmenachDistillery,
Cromdale, Moray*

TYPE	
Single malt	
BOTTLING AGE	
12 years	
STRENGTH	
43%	
TASTE RATING	
4	
MINIATURES	
Yes	
COMMENTS	

The Balmenach Distillery, in the Haughs of Cromdale, is set in an area which was notorious for illicit distilling for many years before the Licensing Act of 1823. Built in 1824 by James McGregor (great-grandfather of Sir Robert Bruce Lockhart, author of the classic 1951 book, *Scotch*), Balmenach was one of the first distilleries in the Highlands to be licensed under the 1823 act. The distillery was acquired by United Distillers and most of its production went into the company's blends but was subsequently closed. It was acquired by Inver House in 1997, restored and re-opened the following year.

A complicated, full-bodied malt best suited as an after-dinner dram. It is available as a single malt only from independent bottlers.

The Balvenie

Balvenie Distillery,
Dufftown, Keith, Banffshire

TYPE
Single malt

BOTTLING AGE
10 years (Founder's Reserve),
12 years (Doublewood),
15 years (Single Barrel),
21 years (Portwood)

STRENGTH
Varies

TASTE RATING
3–4

MINIATURES
Yes

COMMENTS

Founder's Reserve has a rich colour, bouquet and flavour with a smooth, clean, dry finish. Doublewood is full-bodied, yet smooth and mellow, and Single Barrel, which is a harder-to-obtain 15-year-old, is a single-cask bottling.

VISITORS

The distillery is not open to visitors.

*B*uilt in 1892 near the ruins of fourteenth-century Balvenie Castle by the Grants of Glenfiddich, Balvenie Distillery has now been owned by an independent family company for five generations. Balvenie Distillery still grows its own barley, malts in its own traditional floor maltings, employs coopers to tend the barrels and coppersmiths to tend the stills. The Balvenie is most unusual in producing a range of four malt whiskies of different age and character.

Banff

Banff Distillery,
Banff, Banffshire

TYPE
Single malt
BOTTLING AGE
Varies
STRENGTH
Varies
TASTE RATING
2–3
MINIATURES
Yes
COMMENTS

*T*his distillery had an eventful history after its founding in 1863. It survived damage by fire in the 1870s, and was one of the few distilleries to be bombed during the Second World War, when thousands of gallons of whisky had to be thrown away to prevent the spread of fire. It was reported that the whisky running over the land and into nearby streams caused intoxication among the local farm animals and birds, and that dairy cows could not stand up to be milked! The distillery also once supplied whisky to Parliament. It was closed down by its parent company, the Distillers Company Ltd, in 1983, and has since been demolished.

A pleasant, slightly smoky, sweet bouquet leads into a whisky with a rather assertive taste. A rare malt, available from independent merchants only.

Bell's
Extra Special

United Distillers and Vintners, Glasgow

TYPE
Blend

BOTTLING AGE
8 years

STRENGTH
43%

TASTE RATING
2–3

COMMENTS

The most popular blend in the UK, Bell's Extra Special is a pleasant, medium-bodied whisky with a nutty aroma and a spicy flavour.

*T*he merchants and blending company which ultimately became Arthur Bell & Sons was begun in Perth in 1825. Bell himself joined the firm as a traveller in the 1840s and became a partner in 1851. The 'Extra Special' name, accompanied by Bell's signature, was registered as a trade mark in 1895. Large-scale expansion came in the 1930s after the ending of Prohibition in the USA, when Bell acquired three of the company's subsequent complement of five distilleries. Bell's is now owned by United Distillers and Vintners who relaunched Bell's Extra Special as an 8-year-old blend in 1994.

DISTILLED AND BOTTLED IN SCOTLAND

BEN NEVIS

SINGLE HIGHLAND MALT SCOTCH WHISKY

BEN NEVIS DISTILLERY (FORT WILLIAM) LIMITED

DISTILLED IN 1969

75cl   BOTTLED IN 1995   **54.0% vol**

Ben Nevis

Ben Nevis Distillery,
Fort William, Inverness-shire

TYPE
Single malt

BOTTLING AGE
19, 25, 26 years

STRENGTH
Varies

TASTE RATING
3

MINIATURES
No

COMMENTS
Ranging from pale amber to a deep, golden colour, Ben Nevis is characterized by its fresh, slightly peaty flavour and smooth finish.

VISITORS
Visitors are welcome 0900–1700 Mon.–Fri. all year (0900–1730 Jul.–Aug.) and 1000– 1600 Sat., Easter–Sep. Larger parties are advised to telephone 01397-700200 to arrange.

*B*en Nevis Distillery, standing at the foot of Scotland's highest mountain, is one of the oldest distilleries in Scotland. It was founded at Fort William by the famous local character, 'Long' John Macdonald in 1825. (The brand name of Long John and the distillery company became separated.) After more than 100 years and three generations in the family, the distillery was sold in 1941. The subsequent addition of a patent still made the distillery one of the few that could produce both malt and grain under one roof., and it received a new lease of life in the 1980s following its acquisition by the Nikka Whisky Distilling Co. of Japan.

Benriach

Benriach Distillery,
Elgin, Moray

TYPE
Single malt

BOTTLING AGE
10 years

STRENGTH
43%

TASTE RATING
4

MINIATURES
Yes

COMMENTS
A medium-bodied, fruity whisky with sweetish overtones and a gently malty finish. A new bottling has been available from the distillery since 1994.

VISITORS
The distillery is not open to visitors.

BENRIACH DISTILLERY
EST.1898
A SINGLE
PURE HIGHLAND MALT
Scotch Whisky
Benriach Distillery, in the heart of the Highlands, still malts its own barley. The resulting whisky has a unique and attractive delicacy
PRODUCED AND BOTTLED BY THE
BENRIACH
DISTILLERY C⁰
ELGIN, MORAYSHIRE, SCOTLAND, IV30 3SJ
Distilled and Bottled in Scotland
AGED 10 YEARS
70 cl ◆ 43% vol

Originally built in the 1890s, Benriach was closed in 1900, after recession hit the previously booming whisky industry. It was refitted and reopened in 1965, but not completely modernized, still retaining its hand-turned malting floor. The company is owned by Seagram, and most of its produce goes into their blends. Although the distillery now produces its own, official bottling, this is still not an easy whisky to come across.

Benrinnes

Benrinnes Distillery,
Aberlour, Banffshire

TYPE
Single malt

BOTTLING AGE
15 years

STRENGTH
43%

TASTE RATING
4

MINIATURES
Yes

COMMENTS
This is a complex Speyside malt which has hints of wood and grass to its flavour, and a fruity aftertaste.

VISITORS
The distillery is not open to visitors.

*B*uilt almost 700 feet up the slopes of Ben Rinnes, from which it takes its name, this distillery is believed to have been founded in 1835 although evidence exists of distilling on this site in 1826. It was largely rebuilt and modernized in the 1950s. Most of its production is distilled three times rather than the more usual twice, and almost all is used in United Distillers and Vinters' blends. The single malt is still relatively rare, only becoming available in official bottlings in the Distillery (Flora and Fauna) Malts series early in the 1990s.

Benromach

*Benromach Distillery,
Forres, Moray*

TYPE
Single malt

BOTTLING AGE
Varies

STRENGTH
Varies

TASTE RATING
2–3

MINIATURES
Yes

COMMENTS
Subtle and sweet, this Speyside malt has a gentle, fragrant palate and refreshing aftertaste. It is available from independent merchants.

*B*enromach was built just outside Forres in 1898, in the years of expansion for the whisky industry, and it underwent extensive reconstruction in 1966 and 1974. It passed through several hands until coming to rest with the Distillers Company Ltd in 1953. Supplies of the whisky may not be easy to come by for the immediate future, as the distillery was closed from 1983 to 1993, when it was sold by United Distillers to the independent merchants and bottlers Gordon and MacPhail. Since then it has been refitted, and distillation recommenced in 1996.

Black & White

*United Distillers and Vintners,
Banbeath, Leven, Fife*

TYPE	
Blend	
STRENGTH	
40%	
TASTE RATING	
2	
MINIATURES	
Yes	
COMMENTS	

A clean, pleasantly mild blend, Black & White has a fresh, grassy flavour complemented by a light sweetness.

*B*lack & White is the standard blend of the company begun in 1884 by James Buchanan as a whisky blenders and merchants in London. Within a year it was a success, with a contract to supply the House of Commons, and the firm was one of the prime movers in the introduction of blended whiskies to the English market. The whisky was bottled and labelled in a very distinctive black and white livery, and this popular nickname eventually was adopted as the brand name. The company amalgamated with Dewar's in 1915, and both joined the Distillers Company ten years later. Black & White is currently available only outside the UK.

Black Bottle

Allied Distillers,
Dumbarton, Dunbartonshire

TYPE
Blend

STRENGTH
40%

TASTE RATING
2–3

MINIATURES
Yes

COMMENTS

Black Bottle is a superior-quality, smooth blend with a fresh hint of peat, complemented by sweeter, malty notes.

VISITORS

The plant is not suitable for visitors.

*B*lack Bottle was first produced by a family of merchants from Aberdeen in 1879, and has been a premium blend ever since it first appeared on the market. The company was sold to Long John International in 1959, later being acquired by Allied Distillers in 1990, before ultimately passing into the control of Matthew Gloag, the producers of The Famous Grouse blend. A big seller in the Scottish market, Black Bottle is linked to Laphroaig. Its distinctive pot-still-shaped bottle, used almost since its first appearance, rapidly became its trademark and has remained virtually unchanged to the present day.

Black Watch

*Chivas Brothers,
Paisley*

TYPE
Blend

STRENGTH
40%

TASTE RATING
2

MINIATURES
No

COMMENTS
A smooth, mellow blend with a
light, smoky finish.

*C*hivas Brothers is a subsidiary of the Canadian drinks firm Seagram, by whom it was bought in 1949. The origins of the Chivas Brothers company can be traced back to the establishment of a wine and spirit merchant and licensed grocer in Aberdeen in 1801. As the owner of nine distilleries, Seagram is an important company in the Scotch whisky market. Black Watch is one of several Seagram-owned blended whiskies, among which Passport and the de luxe Chivas Regal and Royal Salute are especially well regarded.

Bladnoch

*Bladnoch Distillery, Bladnoch,
Wigtown, Wigtownshire*

TYPE
Single malt

BOTTLING AGE
10 years

STRENGTH
43%

TASTE RATING
3

MINIATURES
Yes

COMMENTS
Bladnoch is a light-to-medium-bodied malt with a light, fragrant, lemony aroma and a gentle, unassertive flavour with fruity tones.

VISITORS
The distillery is not open to visitors.

LOWLAND
SINGLE MALT
SCOTCH WHISKY

The *Broad Leaved Helleborine*,
a rare species of *wild orchid*, can be found growing
in the *ancient oak woodland* behind the

BLADNOCH

distillery. The most southerly in *SCOTLAND*,
founded in the *early* 1800's, *&* the
distillery stands by the *RIVER BLADNOCH*
near *Wigtown*. It produces a *distinctive*
LOWLAND single MALT WHISKY ~ *delicate* and
fruity with a *lemony* aroma and *taste*.

AGED **10** YEARS

43% vol   70 cl

Distilled & Bottled in SCOTLAND
BLADNOCH DISTILLERY, Bladnoch, Wigtownshire, Scotland

*B*ladnoch was Scotland's most southerly distillery, in Wigtownshire, and was also one of its oldest. It was built in 1817 and stood on the banks of the River Bladnoch, in the village of the same name. It had many owners throughout the course of the twentieth century, the latest being United Distillers and Vintners. The distillery is now closed. Bladnoch's single malt is still relatively rare, only becoming available in official bottlings in UDV's Distillery (Flora and Fauna) Malts series early in the 1990s.

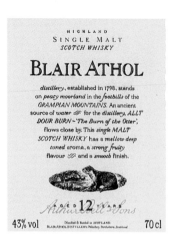

HIGHLAND
SINGLE MALT
SCOTCH WHISKY

BLAIR ATHOL

distillery, established in 1798, stands
on *peaty moorland* in the *foothills* of the
GRAMPIAN MOUNTAINS. An ancient
source of *water* for the *distillery*, *ALLT*
DOUR BURN – *'The Burn of the Otter'*,
flows close by. This *single MALT*
SCOTCH WHISKY has a *mellow deep*
toned aroma, a strong fruity
flavour and a *smooth* finish.

AGED 12 YEARS

43% vol

Distilled & Bottled in SCOTLAND
BLAIR ATHOL DISTILLERY, Pitlochry, Perthshire, Scotland.

70 cl

Blair Athol

Blair Athol Distillery, Pitlochry, Perthshire

TYPE
Single malt

BOTTLING AGE
12 years

STRENGTH
43%

TASTE RATING
2–3

MINIATURES
Yes

COMMENTS
Blair Athol is a light, fresh single malt with dry notes and a hint of smokiness.

VISITORS
Visitors are welcome 0900–1700 Mon.–Sat. and 1200–1700 Sun., Easter–Sept.; 0900–1700 Mon.–Fri., Oct.–Easter. Restricted hours Nov.–Feb. Telephone 01796-482003.

This is a picturesquely sited distillery on a wooded hillside on the outskirts of the pretty Perthshire tourist centre of Pitlochry. Blair Athol is unusual in that it is twelve miles distant from the village after which it is named. Established in 1825, the distillery was bought by Bell in 1933 and sympathetically upgraded. It is now owned by United Distillers and Vintners. Its water comes from the Allt Dour (Burn of the Otter) which flows past the distillery en route to the River Tummel.

Bowmore

Bowmore Distillery,
Bowmore, Islay, Argyll

TYPE
Single malt

BOTTLING AGE
Not specified, 12, 17, 21,
22, 25, 30 years

STRENGTH
40%, 43%

TASTE RATING
3

MINIATURES
Yes

COMMENTS
With its pleasant aroma and peaty–fruity flavour, Bowmore is a good Islay malt for newcomers to these distinctive whiskies to try.

VISITORS
Visitors are welcome. Telephone 01496-810441 to arrange.

$\mathcal{E}$stablished in 1779, Bowmore is reputed to be the oldest legal distillery on Islay. It stands in the island's main town and overlooks Loch Indaal, and its water is taken from the peaty River Laggan. The distillery has passed through several hands in the twentieth century, but it has been a consistently thriving concern since its acquisition in 1963 by Stanley P. Morrison of Glasgow. The company is now Morrison Bowmore Distillers Ltd, and this is their flagship distillery.

Bruichladdich

Bruichladdich Distillery,
Bruichladdich, Islay,
Argyll

TYPE	
Single malt	
BOTTLING AGE	
10, 15, 21 years	
STRENGTH	
40%	
TASTE RATING	
3	
MINIATURES	
Yes	
COMMENTS	

Built in 1881, Bruichladdich is Scotland's most westerly distillery. Its water comes from an inland reservoir and, unlike the other distilleries, is not drawn from springs which have flowed over peaty land; this has been suggested as a reason why its peaty flavour is less intense than other Islay malts. Bruichladdich was owned by Invergordon Distillers from 1972 until 1993, but since the company's acquisition that year by Whyte & Mackay, it has been moth-balled along with two of the group's other distilleries, Tamnavulin and Tullibardine.

A subtle malt, and less medicinal in its flavour than other Islay whiskies, Bruichladdich is a lightish, dry, fresh-tasting whisky.

Bunnahabhain

*Bunnahabhain Distillery,
Port Askaig, Islay, Argyll*

TYPE
Single malt

BOTTLING AGE
12 years

STRENGTH
40%

TASTE RATING
3–4

MINIATURES
Yes

COMMENTS
Less characteristically peaty
than some other Islay malts,
Bunnahabhain is a mellow
whisky with an aromatic
flavour.

VISITORS
Visitors welcome by appointment. Telephone 01496-840646
to arrange.

*B*unnahabhain, on the north
shore of Islay, is one of the
more isolated of the island's distilleries. Founded in 1881, it has changed
very little in the intervening century
despite expansion in the 1960s. All its
production formerly went into blends.
Bunnahabhain was owned by the Islay
Distillery Company who bought Glen
Rothes Distillery in 1887, which
together formed the Highland
Distilleries Company. They still own
Bunnahabhain today.

Cameron Brig

Cameronbridge Distillery,
Cameron Bridge, Fife

TYPE

Grain

STRENGTH

40%

TASTE RATING

1

MINIATURES

Yes

COMMENTS

Like other grain whiskies, a lighter spirit than malt, with a fresh taste and an element of smoothness.

VISITORS

The distillery is not open to visitors.

*C*ameronbridge Distillery had been operating for several years before it was acquired in 1824 by John Haig, one of the famous family of Lowland whisky distillers. One of its most famous directors, who subsequently became a director at the Distillers Company Ltd, was Field Marshal Douglas Haig, commander-in-chief of the British Army on the Western Front during the First World War. Haig's company was among the founders of the Distillers Company in 1877, and United Distillers and Vintners still own the distillery today. Cameronbridge produced both grain and malt whisky using a mixture of pot and patent stills until 1929 before finally concentrating on grain alone.

Caol Ila

Caol Ila Distillery,
Port Askaig, Islay, Argyll

TYPE

Single malt

BOTTLING AGE

15 years

STRENGTH

43%

TASTE RATING

4

MINIATURES

Yes

COMMENTS

Nicely balanced, Caol Ila is not the most peaty of the Islay whiskies, but is pleasantly dry with a well-rounded body.

VISITORS

Visitors are welcome Mon.–Fri. by appointment. Telephone 01496-302760 to arrange.

*C*aol Ila was established in 1846 and overlooks the Sound of Islay (which is also the English translation of its name). It previously used its own wharf for transporting its product. The distillery has been rebuilt twice, at almost 100-year intervals, in 1879 and 1972. The most recent modernization almost doubled the distillery's output. Caol Ila is now owned by United Distillers and Vintners. The single malt is still relatively rare, only becoming available in official bottlings in UDV's Distillery (Flora and Fauna) Malts series early in the 1990s.

Caperdonich

*Caperdonich Distillery,
Rothes, Moray*

TYPE

Single malt

BOTTLING AGE

Varies

STRENGTH

Varies

TASTE RATING

3

MINIATURES

Yes

COMMENTS

A pleasant Speyside malt of light-to-medium body, with a delicately fruity flavour combined with a hint of peat.

VISITORS

The distillery is not open to visitors.

*O*riginally owned by J & J Grant, this distillery was built across the road from their main production centre at Glen Grant. The two distilleries were to be treated as one for licensing purposes, so a pipe spanned the road to carry the produce of Caperdonich (then known as Glen Grant Number Two) across for blending. Built to take advantage of the boom years of the 1890s, it suffered with the fall-off in consumption and was closed in the early 1900s, waiting over sixty years for renovation and reopening under the new name of Caperdonich. Most of its produce goes into blends, with only some available from independent merchants.

Cardhu

Cardhu Distillery,
Knockando, Moray

TYPE
Single malt

BOTTLING AGE
12 years

STRENGTH
40%

TASTE RATING
2–3

MINIATURES
Yes

COMMENTS
A smooth, light malt of silky character and delicate, sweet flavour which make it accessible to all from the novice to the connoisseur.

VISITORS
Visitors are welcome 0930–1630 Mon.–Fri. Mar.–Nov.; also 0930–1630 Sat. and 1100–1600 Sun. Jul.–Sept.; 1000–1600 Mon.–Fri. Dec.–Feb. Telephone 01340-872555

*W*hisky distilling had been carried on illegally in this area for a long time before Cardow Distillery, as it was then, was founded and licensed in 1824. The distillery was bought by John Walker of Kilmarnock during the boom years of the 1890s, producing a vatted and a single malt under the Cardhu name. It was modernized in 1965 and its single malt was relaunched, with the distillery name being changed in 1981 to match that of its product. It is now owned by United Distillers and Vintners. Cardhu enjoys a splendid situation overlooking the Spey valley and has recently been refurbished.

Chivas Regal

Chivas Brothers,
Paisley, Renfrewshire

TYPE
De luxe

BOTTLING AGE
12, 18 years

STRENGTH
40%

TASTE RATING
2–3

MINIATURES
Yes

COMMENTS
A classic de luxe blend with a malty sweetness and a trace of peatiness in its flavours.

*C*hivas Brothers is a subsidiary of the Canadian drinks firm Seagram, by whom it was bought in 1949. The origins of the Chivas Brothers company can be traced back to the establishment of a wine and spirit merchant and licensed grocer in Aberdeen in 1801. Owning nine malt distilleries, Seagram is an important company in the Scotch whisky market. Chivas Regal is one of several Seagram blends which include Passport, Black Watch and the premium 21-year-old Royal Salute.

The Claymore

JBB (Greater Europe) plc, Glasgow

TYPE

Blend

STRENGTH

40%

TASTE RATING

2–3

MINIATURES

Yes

COMMENTS

A nicely rounded, medium-bodied blend with a mellow aroma and a well-balanced, smooth and rich taste.

VISITORS

The blending and bottling plant is not open to visitors.

*T*he Claymore is a popular blend which is owned by JBB (Greater Europe), formerly Whyte & Mackay, the blending and bottling company begun in 1882 by whisky merchants James Whyte and Charles Mackay. A blend of up to 35 diffrent malt and grain whiskies from the Highland, Island and Lowlands whisky regions of Scotland, The Claymore is successful in export markets as well as in the UK, where it is among the best-selling blends.

Clynelish

*Clynelish Distillery,
Brora, Sutherland*

TYPE
Single malt

BOTTLING AGE
14 years

STRENGTH
43%

TASTE RATING
3

MINIATURES
Yes

COMMENTS

Clynelish is a medium-bodied, full-flavoured whisky with many devotees. It is slightly dry to the taste, with a hint of peat.

VISITORS

Visitors are welcome 0930– 1630 Mon.–Fri., Mar.–Oct.; 0930– 1600 Tue.–Thur., Nov.– Feb. or by appointment. Telephone 01408-623014.

*T*his distillery had its origins in the early nineteenth century and was built by the man who became the first Duke of Sutherland, the prime mover in the most infamous of the Highland Clearances. Its purpose was to make full use of the cheap grain grown on the new coastal farms of his newly-cleared tenants. The distillery was bought by Ainslie and Heilbron in 1896. A new distillery was built on adjacent land in 1967–68, taking the name Clynelish, while the original distillery, now renamed Brora, was closed by the Distillers Company Ltd, its parent company, in 1983. It is now owned by United Distillers and Vintners.

Coleburn

Coleburn Distillery,
Longmorn, Elgin, Moray

TYPE
Single malt

BOTTLING AGE
Varies

STRENGTH
Varies

TASTE RATING
3

MINIATURES
Yes

COMMENTS
A difficult-to-find malt with a delicate, fragrant aroma and pleasant, slightly flowery taste. Available bottled by independent merchants.

*C*oleburn was built by John Robertson of Dundee in 1896 and was licensed to J. & G. Stewart, a subsidiary of the Distillers Company Ltd and blenders of Usher's whiskies. It was acquired by United Distillers and mothballed in 1985. Almost all of its produce went into blends, and since its closure, its malt has become even rarer.

Columba Cream

John Murray & Co (Mull),
Calgary, Isle of Mull

TYPE

Liqueur

BOTTLING AGE

4 years

STRENGTH

17%

TASTE RATING

2

MINIATURES

Yes

COMMENTS

A blend of five single malt whiskies, with the addition of honey and cream makes for a very pleasant and mellow whisky cream liqueur.

VISITORS

The plant is not open to visitors.

John Murray & Co. have been producing Columba Cream for several years to a formula which is based on a traditional recipe. With five single malts included in its recipe, this high-quality cream liqueur is an exceptionally fine example of its type. The company has offices on the Isle of Mull, and blending and bottling is currently carried out at their plant in Perth.

Convalmore

*Convalmore Distillery,
Dufftown, Keith, Banffshire*

TYPE
Single malt

BOTTLING AGE
Varies

STRENGTH
Varies

TASTE RATING
3

MINIATURES
Yes

COMMENTS
Available only from independent merchants, this is a dry, aromatic, atypical Speyside malt which works best as a digestif.

W. P. Lowrie, the present licensed distillers, bought Convalmore in 1904, eleven years after its founding. Considerably damaged by fire in 1909, it was rebuilt the following year when experiments were made in the production of malt whisky from patent stills; this was abandoned in 1916, however, in favour of the traditional pot-still method which was considered to mature the whisky better. Almost all the production of Convalmore goes into blends. The distillery is now owned by William Grant & Sons and was mothballed in 1985.

Cragganmore

Cragganmore Distillery, Ballindalloch, Banffshire

TYPE	
Single malt	
BOTTLING AGE	
12 years	
STRENGTH	
40%	
TASTE RATING	
3–4	
MINIATURES	
Yes	

COMMENTS

Cragganmore is a Speyside malt of distinctive and complex character, with a delicate aroma and smoky finish.

VISITORS

The distillery is not open to visitors except for Friends of the Classic Malts, who can visit by appointment.

*C*ragganmore was built in 1869 and was the first distillery to be constructed alongside an existing railway and so utilise the then new mode of transport for distribution. The distillery took its name from nearby Craggan More Hill. It was built by John Smith (a man of great bulk, also known locally as 'Cragganmore') and is now licensed to D. & J. McCallum. Most of its production goes into blends, especially Old Parr, and until a few years ago, the single malt was only infrequently available. The distillery is owned by United Distillers and Vintners.

Craigellachie

*Craigellachie Distillery,
Craigellachie, Aberlour,
Banffshire*

SPEYSIDE
SINGLE MALT
SCOTCH WHISKY

CRAIGELLACHIE

distillery, founded in 1888, in the *county of*
BANFFSHIRE, stands *overlooking* the
RIVER SPEY, the rock *of Craigellachie*, and
TELFORD'S single span iron BRIDGE. The
distillery uses local *spring water* running from
little *CONVAL HILL* for mashing, *resulting*
in this excellent *single MALT SCOTCH*
WHISKY *of light and* smoky character.

AGED **14** YEARS

43% vol   Distilled & Bottled in SCOTLAND
CRAIGELLACHIE DISTILLERY
Craigellachie, Banffshire, Scotland   70 cl

TYPE
Single malt

BOTTLING AGE
14 years

STRENGTH
43%

TASTE RATING
3

MINIATURES
Yes

COMMENTS
A smoky-smelling and -tasting malt of medium body, Craigellachie works well as an after-dinner dram. It is generally available from independent whisky merchants.

VISITORS
The distillery is not open to visitors.

*T*his distillery is pleasantly situated on high ground above the River Spey outside Dufftown. It was built in 1891 by the Craigellachie Distillery Co., a founder of which was Peter Mackie, the creator of the White Horse brand. Mackie and Co. (later White Horse Distillers) subsequently bought the distillery in 1915. Owned by United Distillers, most of its production was devoted to blending. The single malt is still relatively rare, only becoming available in official bottlings in the Distillery (Flora and Fauna) Malts series early in the 1990s. It is now owned by John Dewar and Sons.

Crawford's
Three Star

JBB (Greater Europe) plc, Glasgow

TYPE
Blend

STRENGTH
40%

TASTE RATING
2

MINIATURES
Yes

COMMENTS
A smooth, nicely balanced blend with light, malty flavours.

A & A. Crawford was established as a whisky merchant and blenders in Leith in 1860. Although the original founders died before the end of the century, the business was taken over by their sons who were responsible for the launching of the successful Crawford's Three Star blend at the start of the century. A de luxe Five Star appeared in the 1920s and was also well received. A. & A. Crawford was acquired by the Distillers Company Ltd in 1944 and ownership subsequently passed to Whyte & Mackay in 1986, which in turn became JBB (Greater Europe).

Cutty Sark

Berry Brothers & Rudd Ltd,
London

TYPE

Blend

STRENGTH

40%

TASTE RATING

2

MINIATURES

Yes

COMMENTS

A delicate, smooth whisky with a fresh, crisp taste. A high proportion of oak-matured Speyside malts contributes greatly to its smooth taste.

erry Brothers & Rudd, have been successful London wine and spirit merchants since the seventeenth century. Their Cutty Sark blend was launched in 1923 specifically for the American market, where it quickly became a brand leader, a position it has sustained ever since. It is also a leading premium blend in countries such as Greece, Japan, Portugal, Korea and Brazil. The whisky takes its name from the famous clipper ship built in Scotland in 1869, renowned as one of the fastest sailing ships of its day. The distinctive yellow label was designed by the Scottish artist, James McBey.

Cutty Sark Emerald

Berry Brothers & Rudd Ltd,
London

TYPE

Blend

STRENGTH

43%

TASTE RATING

2

MINIATURES

Yes

COMMENTS

Cutty Sark Emerald has a soft, honeyed fruit aroma, a hint of sweetness on the palate and a rounded, lengthy finish.

*B*erry Brothers & Rudd have been successful London wine and spirit merchants since the seventeenth century. The original Cutty Sark blend was launched in 1923 specifically for the American market, where it quickly became a brand leader, a position it has sustained ever since. A blend of oak-matured whiskies of at least 12 years of age, Cutty Sark Emerald has strong international following, particularly in Japan, Korea, Portugal, Spain and Greece.

Cutty Sark
Imperial Kingdom Golden Jubilee

Berry Brothers & Rudd Ltd, London

TYPE	
Blend	
STRENGTH	
43%	
TASTE RATING	
2–3	
MINIATURES	
No	

COMMENTS

Exceptionally smooth, Golden Jubilee is a rich, fruity nosed whisky with a slightly sweet taste and a lingering finish.

*B*erry Brothers & Rudd have been successful London wine and spirit merchants since the seventeenth century. The original Cutty Sark blend was launched in 1923 specifically for the American market, where it quickly became a brand leader, a position it has sustained ever since. Imperial Kingdom Golden Jubilee is produced from Berry Bros & Rudd's own private whisky reserves and contains a some very fine rare whiskies over 50-years-old. Golden Jubilee is a commemoration of Queen Victoria's reign and the handsome gift-box packaging illustrates the achievements of that age.

Dailuaine

Dailulaine Distillery,
Carron, Banffshire

SPEYSIDE
SINGLE MALT *SCOTCH WHISKY*

DAILUAINE

is the GAELIC for "the green vale". The *distillery* established
in 1852, lies in a hollow by the *CARRON BURN* in *BANFFSHIRE*. This
single Malt Scotch Whisky has a *full bodied fruity nose* and a *smoky finish*.
For more than a *hundred years* all *distillery supplies* were despatched by
rail. The *steam locomotive* "DAILUAINE NO.1" was in use
from 1939 – 1967 and is preserved on the *STRATHSPEY RAILWAY*.

A G E D **16** Y E A R S

43% vol   Distilled & Bottled in SCOTLAND. DAILUAINE DISTILLERY, Carron, Aberlour, Banffshire, Scotland.   70 cl

TYPE	
Single malt	
BOTTLING AGE	
16 years	
STRENGTH	
43%	
TASTE RATING	
4	
MINIATURES	
Yes	

COMMENTS

This is a rare malt, with a heathery and sweetish flavour.

VISITORS

The distillery is not open to visitors.

*D*ailuaine Distillery stands near the Spey below Ben Rinnes and was established in 1851 by William Mackenzie; it was subsequently taken over by his son, Thomas, and greatly expanded during the 1880s. The distillery was one of several owned by the Dailuaine–Talisker Distillery Co., an amalgamated company formed by Mackenzie. Its current owners are United Distillers and Vintners and most of its produce goes into their blends, such as Johnnie Walker. Consequently, its single malt is still relatively rare, and has only become available in official bottlings in the Distillery (Flora and Fauna) Malts series early in the 1990s.

The Dalmore

Dalmore Distillery,
Alness, Ross-shire

TYPE
Single malt

BOTTLING AGE
12 years

STRENGTH
40%

TASTE RATING
4

MINIATURES
Yes

COMMENTS
A smooth, full-bodied whisky with a hint of sherry and peat in its malted flavours. A good digestif.

VISITORS
Visitors are welcome by appointment at 1100 or 1400 Mon., Tue., Thur., early Sept.–mid-June. Telephone 01349-882362 to arrange.

*B*uilt in 1839, Dalmore Distillery was bought in 1867 by the Mackenzie family, although ownership passed to Whyte & Mackay (and subsequently to its commercial successor, JBB). Much of its produce today goes into JBB blends. The distillery is attractively set in a picturesque location with a wooded, hilly backdrop and outlook over the Cromarty Firth to the fertile Black Isle. This location led to a break in the production of whisky during the First World War when the American navy took over the distillery and its access to the deepwater Cromarty Firth for the manufacture of mines.

Dalwhinnie

Dalwhinnie Distillery,
Dalwhinnie, Inverness-shire

TYPE
Single malt

BOTTLING AGE
15 years

STRENGTH
43%

TASTE RATING
2–3

MINIATURES
Yes

COMMENTS

Ideal as a pre- or post-dinner dram, Dalwhinnie is light and aromatic with a soft, heather-honey finish.

VISITORS

Visitors are welcome 0930–1630, Mon.–Fri., Mar.–Dec.; also 0930–1630 Sat., Jan.–Oct. and 1230–1630 Jul.–Aug. Telephone 01540-672219.

*B*uilt in 1898 at the end of the boom years for the whisky industry, what is today Dalwhinnie Distillery was called Strathspey when it first opened, even though it was not, strictly speaking, on Speyside. It stands on the Drumochter Pass at a height of over 1000 feet, close to pure water sources, and was for many years Scotland's highest distillery. It is owned by United Distillers and Vintners. Most of its output went to blending until 1988 when the Dalwhinnie single malt was developed.

Deanston

Deanston Distillery,
Doune, Perthshire

TYPE

Single malt

BOTTLING AGE

12, 17 years

STRENGTH

40%

TASTE RATING

3

MINIATURES

Yes

COMMENTS

A light, fresh, smooth Highland malt with a sweetish, fruity flavour.

VISITORS

The distillery is not open to visitors.

*O*riginally a cotton mill dating back to 1785, Deanston was converted to a whisky distillery in 1966. Water for distilling and electricity comes from the River Teith that rises north of Loch Lomond and flows through the Trossachs. The mill's original weaving sheds, with their humidity control and their temperature, are perfect for maturing the whisky and are considered to add a natural smoothness to its character. Deanston was bought by Burn Stewart of Glasgow in 1991 and its malt is a major component of the Wallace liqueur.

Dewar's White Label

John Dewar & Sons, Glasgow

TYPE
Blend

STRENGTH
40%

TASTE RATING
2

MINIATURES
Yes

COMMENTS

Dewar's White Label, the best-selling Scotch whisky in the USA, has a slightly smoky aroma and a complex, delicate, malty flavour with a clean, dry finish.

*J*ohn Dewar and Sons was one of the blending companies instrumental in the development of new whisky markets outside Scotland. Begun in Perth in 1846, it was the first company to sell its whisky in bottles as well as casks, thus opening up a new market in the home rather than just the licensed shop, pub or hotel. Dewar was also a pioneer of whisky advertising and was one of the first companies whose bottles carried its company name. By the time it became part of the Distillers Company Ltd in 1925, it owned seven distilleries including Aberfeldy which produces the malt at the heart of Dewar's blends. More than 90% of the company's production is exported.

Dimple

*United Distillers,
Banbeath, Leven, Fife*

TYPE
De luxe

BOTTLING AGE
15 years

STRENGTH
40%

TASTE RATING
2–3

MINIATURES
Yes

COMMENTS

In its distinctive triangular bottle, Dimple is a good-quality de luxe blend which is also a leader in its market in the UK. More sophisticated than the standard Haig blend, it has a mellow sweetness which is harmoniously balanced by a smoky, peaty flavour.

*H*aig is a family name long associated with the whisky industry, going back almost 350 years, when Robert Haig, a farmer of Stirlingshire, was rebuked by his local kirk session for distilling his whisky on a Sunday. The Haigs were instrumental in introducing new practices and machinery (for example the new patent still in the 1830s) to the grain distilleries which they built in Edinburgh and elsewhere in the east. The company was acquired by the Distillers Company in 1919 and by United Distillers in 1986. Today Haig holds the licence for three malt distilleries: Glenkinchie, Glenlossie and Mannochmore, as well as Cameronbridge grain distillery in Fife.

Drambuie

Drambuie,
Kirkliston, West Lothian

TYPE	
Liqueur	
STRENGTH	
40%	
TASTE RATING	
2	
MINIATURES	
Yes	

COMMENTS

A blend of secret ingredients, Drambuie is a sweet after-dinner whisky liqueur with a rich and creamy honeyed flavour complemented by fragrant, fruity notes.

VISITORS

The plant is not open to visitors.

*D*rambuie is produced in the Lothians, having moved from its original home on Skye at the start of this century after the decision was taken to produce the liqueur commercially. Drambuie ('the drink that satisfies') is chronicled – perhaps with a keener eye on marketing than history – as being the personal liqueur of Prince Charles Edward Stuart, Bonnie Prince Charlie. After his army's defeat by the Hanoverian army at Culloden in 1746, the prince fled to Skye with a few supporters. Among them was Captain John Mackinnon, a native of Skye, whom the prince is said to have rewarded for his loyalty by giving him his only remaining possession – the secret recipe for his personal liqueur.

Dufftown

Dufftown Distillery,
Dufftown, Keith, Banffshire

TYPE
Single malt

BOTTLING AGE
15 years

STRENGTH
43%

TASTE RATING
2–3

MINIATURES
Yes

COMMENTS
A pleasant Speyside malt with a delicate, fragrant aroma which is almost flowery, and a smooth, sweet taste. Doubles as a before- or after-dinner dram.

VISITORS
Visitors are welcome by appointment, 0900–1600. Larger parties should telephone in advance. Telephone 01340-820224 to arrange.

HIGHLAND
SINGLE MALT SCOTCH WHISKY

DUFFTOWN

distillery was established near Dufftown at the end of the C19th. The bright flash of the KINGFISHER can often be seen over the DULLAN RIVER, which flows past the old stone buildings of the distillery on its way north to the SPEY. This single HIGHLAND MALT WHISKY is typically SPEYSIDE in character with a delicate, fragrant, almost flowery aroma and taste which lingers on the palate.

AGED 15 YEARS

43% vol   Distilled & Bottled in SCOTLAND. DUFFTOWN DISTILLERY, Dufftown, Keith, Banffshire, Scotland   70 cl

*P*rettily situated at the water's edge in the Dullan Glen, this is one of seven distilleries in and around Dufftown, a major whisky production centre with plentiful resources of water, peat and, previously, barley. Despite the abundance of fresh water in the glen, there were disputes in the early years over water rights, some of which led to the nocturnal diversion and re-diversion of local supplies. The distillery finally gained the right to draw its supplies from Jock's Well, a reliable source of fine, sweet water some distance away. The single malt is still relatively rare, becoming more widely available in official bottlings in United Distillers' Distillery (Flora and Fauna) Malts series early in the 1990s.

Dunhill Old Master

Justerini & Brooks, London

TYPE
Blend

STRENGTH
43%

TASTE RATING
3

MINIATURES
Yes

COMMENTS

*J*usterini & Brooks' was established in London by the Italian wine merchant, Giacomo Justerini, in 1749 and began selling Scotch whisky thirty years later. In 1962 the company built on previous amalgamations by combining with W. & A. Gilbey to form International Distillers and Vintners Ltd (IDV). Grand Metropolitan bought IDV, then part of Watney Mann & Truman, in 1972. J&B have created a range of high-quality premium whiskies for Alfred Dunhill Ltd, including Dunhill Centenary, Dunhill's Celebration Edition and Dunhill's Gentlemen's Speyside Blend.

A combination of some thirty individual whiskies, some more than twenty years old, Dunhill Old Master is an exceptionally smooth, richly flav-oured blend.

Dunkeld *Atholl Brose*

Gordon and MacPhail,
Elgin, Moray

TYPE

Liqueur

BOTTLING AGE

12 years

STRENGTH

35%

TASTE RATING

2

MINIATURES

Yes

COMMENTS

Based on a traditional recipe, this liqueur has a good whisky association coming through its sweetness. It is herbal on the nose, with a long, warming finish.

VISITORS

Gordon and MacPhail's shop, South St, Elgin is open 0900–1715 Mon.–Wed. (0900–1300 Wed. in winter), 0830–1715 Thu.–Fri., 0900–1700 Sat.

Gordon and MacPhail started in business in 1895 as a licensed grocers and wine and spirit merchant. Unlike many similar contemporary companies, they have retained all the original aspects of their business as well as extending into vatting, blending and bottling, and are unique in maturing all their whiskies from new. They recently moved into distillation with the purchase of Benromach Distillery from United Distillers. They also produce this liqueur, which won a Silver Award (1985) at the International Wine and Spirit Competition and a Gold Award (1987), when it was named 'the best liqueur in the world'.

Edradour

*Edradour Distillery,
Pitlochry, Perthshire*

TYPE
Single malt

BOTTLING AGE
10 years

STRENGTH
40%, 43%

TASTE RATING
3

MINIATURES
Yes

COMMENTS
Edradour is a smooth Highland malt with pleasant notes of fruit and malt in its taste, and is complemented by a slight dryness.

VISITORS
Visitors are welcome. Telephone 01796-472095 to arrange.

*E*dradour is Scotland's smallest distillery, as well as being one of its most picturesque. Built in 1837, it stands on the steep banks of a burn in the Perthshire countryside, and sympathetic modernization in 1982 left its appearance unchanged. The distillery had been bought by William Whiteley in 1933 and, despite a takeover in 1982 by Pernod Ricard subsidiary the House of Campbell, Whiteley still hold the licence. Most of the malt goes into their House of Lords and Clan Campbell blends, and it is only since 1986 that Edradour has been available as a single malt under the distillery label.

Fairlie's

*Glenturret Distillery,
The Hosh, Perthshire*

TYPE

Liqueur

BOTTLING AGE

24%

TASTE RATING

2

MINIATURES

No

COMMENTS

Smooth and delicate without being cloying, the secret recipe used to produce this unique drink allows the top-grade malt used to come through. Excellent as a mixer.

VISITORS

Visitors are welcome all year. Telephone 01764-656565

Fairlie's Light Highland Liqueur is produced at Glenturret Distillery, situated in one of Perthshire's most spectacular Highland settings. It is named after the family which did so much to resurrect the distillery's fortunes in the 1960s. The label sports a pouncing cat motif and paw prints in honour of Towser, the late distillery cat whose record of 28,899 mice caught in a career lasting almost twenty-four years earned her a place in the *Guinness Book of Records* as the world's most successful mouser.

The Famous Grouse

Matthew Gloag & Son,
Perth, Perthshire

TYPE	
Blend	
STRENGTH	
40%	
TASTE RATING	
2	
MINIATURES	
Yes	
COMMENTS	

The Famous Grouse is a light-to-medium-bodied whisky with a fresh smoothness and a pleasant, lightly peated flavour. It has been the most popular blend in Scotland for several years.

Matthew Gloag & Son began trading in Perth in 1800 as a licensed grocers, acquiring interests in blending and bottling as the firm expanded during the nineteenth century. What became their most famous product appeared at the end of the century, with the grouse on the name and label successfully capitalizing on the popularity of sporting pastimes among Victorian and Edwardian gentlemen. The blend celebrated its first century in 1996. The company was bought by Highland Distilleries (now Highland Distillers) in 1970 and received the benefits of wider distribution and advertising. Highland Distillers own Bunnahabhain, Glen Rothes, Glen Turret, Highland Park, The Macallan and Tamdhu malt distilleries.

Fraser McDonald

Gibson Scotch Whisky Ltd, Glasgow

TYPE

Blend

STRENGTH

40%

TASTE RATING

2–3

MINIATURES

No

COMMENTS

Fraser McDonald is a smooth and mellow blend whose light, fresh taste is underlain by gentle peaty notes.

*F*raser McDonald is, along with Scotia Royale and Royal Culross, one of the blends of Gibson Scotch Whisky Co. Ltd, who operate as a subsidiary of the Loch Lomond Distillery Co. Ltd, producers of Inchmurrin, Loch Lomond and Old Rhosdu single malts. As well as a new grain complex at Loch Lomond, the company holds three malt distilleries: the two Lowland distilleries of Loch Lomond at Alexandria and Littlemill at Bowling, and Glen Scotia in Campbeltown. Littlemill is mothballed but Glen Scotia was brought back into production in May 1999.

Glayva

JBB (Greater Europe) plc, Glasgow

TYPE

Liqueur

STRENGTH

35%

BOTTLING AGE

2

MINIATURES

Yes

COMMENTS

*G*layva was originally created by Ronald Morrison & Co., an Edinburgh wine merchants well versed in flavours and bouquets. The liqueur's distinctive combination of aged whisky, syrup of herbs, aromatic oils and honey took many years to perfect. The ownership of Glayva has passed to JBB (Greater Europe), the commercial successor of Whyte & Mackay. Whyte & Mackay secured control of the brand in 1993 when they acquired Invergordon Distillers, who had owned Glayva since 1984. This is one of the biggest sellers in the Scotch whisky liqueur market.

Glayva, whose name derives from the Gaelic for 'very good', is a rich, syrupy-textured after-dinner liqueur with a hint of tangerine in its sweet flavours.

VISITORS

The plant is not open to visitors.

Glen Albyn

Glen Albyn Distillery,
Inverness, Inverness-shire

TYPE
Single malt

STRENGTH
Varies

BOTTLING AGE
Varies

TASTE RATING
3

MINIATURES
Yes

COMMENTS
This whisky is available from independent bottlers only and is difficult to come by. It is a medium-bodied, smooth malt with a hint of smokiness in its bouquet and taste.

Glen Albyn was first established by a provost of Inverness in 1840, only to be turned into a flour mill after two decades of distilling. It was re-established in the 1880s when a new Glen Albyn Distillery was built in another site close to the Caledonian Canal. The distillery was bought by Mackinlay and Birnie (who also owned the neighbouring Glen Mhor Distillery) in 1920 and was transferred to Scottish Malt Distillers (SMD), a subsidiary of the Distillers Company Ltd, in 1972. Glen Albyn was one of several SMD distilleries closed down in 1983 and it was subsequently demolished by United Distillers in 1988.

Glenburgie

*The Glenburgie-Glenlivet
Distillery,
Forres, Moray*

TYPE

Single malt

STRENGTH

Varies

BOTTLING AGE

Varies

TASTE RATING

3

MINIATURES

Yes

COMMENTS

A light-bodied, delicate single malt whose sweet, slightly floral taste makes it ideal as an aperitif. It is found relatively rarely in this country, as most goes for export.

VISITORS

The distillery has no reception centre but visitors are welcome by appointment. Telephone 01343-850258 to arrange.

A distillery was said to have been established here in 1810, but production ceased and was not revived until the second half of the nineteenth century. It was bought by James & George Stodart Ltd of Dumbarton who themselves were taken over by Hiram Walker in the 1930s. The distillery was extended in 1958 and is now owned by Allied Distillers, with most of its produce going into their blends. However, it is still available from independent bottlers.

Glencadam

Glencadam Distillery,
Brechin, Angus

TYPE

Single malt

STRENGTH

Varies

BOTTLING AGE

Varies

TASTE RATING

3–4

MINIATURES

Yes

COMMENTS

Glencadam, generally available from independent whisky merchants, has a delicate, fruity bouquet and rich, sweetish flavour with a smooth, well-rounded finish.

VISITORS

The distillery has no reception centre but visitors are welcome by appointment. Telephone 01356-622217 to arrange.

*G*lencadam, built around 1825, dates from the time of the first wave of licensed distilleries, and was one of two distilleries in Brechin dating from this decade (North Port being the other). It takes its water from Moorfoot Loch. It is owned by Allied Distillers but has only rarely been officially bottled as a single malt, with most of its production going into the Stewarts Cream of the Barley blend.

Glen Calder

*Gordon and MacPhail,
Elgin, Moray*

TYPE

Blend

STRENGTH

40%

TASTE RATING

2

MINIATURES

Yes

COMMENTS

A very pleasant blend with a smooth, honey-like nose and light, slightly smoky finish. This blend has an unusually high proportion of malt whisky.

VISITORS

Gordon and MacPhail's shop, South St, Elgin is open 0900–1715 Mon.–Wed. (0900–1300 Wed. in winter), 0830–1715 Thu.–Fri., 0900–1700 Sat. Telephone 01340-871471.

*G*ordon and MacPhail started in business in 1895 as a licensed grocers and wine and spirit merchant, as had done so many of the foremost names among the Scotch whisky blending industry. Unlike the others, however, Gordon and MacPhail have retained all the original aspects of their business as well as extending into vatting, blending and bottling, and they are today the world's leading malt whisky specialists. Some of the formulas for their blends date from the turn of the century. Glen Calder is one of the most popular blends in northern Scotland and won a Silver Award at the 1981 International Wine and Spirits Competition.

Glen Deveron

Macduff Distillery,
Banff, Banffshire

TYPE
Single malt

BOTTLING AGE
10 years

STRENGTH
40%

TASTE RATING
3–4

MINIATURES
Yes

COMMENTS
A very pleasant Highland malt with a smooth, mellow taste and fresh bouquet.

VISITORS
Visitors are welcome by appointment. Telephone 01261-812612 to arrange.

A modern distillery, built in 1960, Macduff is one of the few distilleries to give its single malt a different name from its own (although independent bottlers do market the whisky, including miniatures, under the name of 'Macduff'). The malt takes its names from the nearby River Deveron from which is drawn the water used for cooling in the production process. Macduff Distillery is now owned by William Lawson Distillers, a subsidiary of Bacardi Ltd, Bermuda.

Glendronach

*The Glendronach Distillery,
Forgue, Huntly,
Aberdeenshire*

TYPE
Single malt
BOTTLING AGE
15 years
STRENGTH
40%, 43%
TASTE RATING
3
MINIATURES
Yes
COMMENTS

*T*his distillery, set picturesquely on the Dronach Burn in the Aberdeenshire countryside, is one of the most attractive in the Highlands. Built in 1826, it was one of the first to be licensed, and its whisky enjoyed a wide reputation in the nineteenth century. Its original hand-turned malting floor and coal-fired stills have been retained. Since 1960 it has been operated by William Teacher & Sons, with produce going into the Teacher's blends. It has been owned since 1988 by Allied Distillers who have temporarily suspended production.

Glendronach is a beautifully rich and smooth malt whose slight peaty tones are balanced by a burst of sherried sweetness.

VISITORS

Visitors are welcome by appointment. Telephone 01466-730202 to arrange.

Glendullan

Glendullan Distillery,
Dufftown, Keith, Banffshire

TYPE

Single malt

BOTTLING AGE

12 years

STRENGTH

43%

TASTE RATING

3

MINIATURES

Yes

COMMENTS

A good single malt with a robust character yet a mellow, fruity flavour.

VISITORS

The distillery is not open to visitors.

*T*his is one of the seven Dufftown distilleries, built just before the turn of the century and picturesquely set on the banks of the Fiddich. Built for William Williams of Aberdeen, it passed to the control of Macdonald Greenlees & Williams after the First World War and, with its parent company, into the ownership of the Distillers Company Ltd in 1926. It is now owned by United Distillers and Vintners and its single malt is still relatively rare, although it has been officially bottled in the Distillery (Flora and Fauna) Malts series. Glendullan is also an important component of Old Parr and of President, a de luxe blend.

Glenfarclas

Glenfarclas Distillery, Marypark, Ballindalloch, Banffshire

TYPE
Single malt
BOTTLING AGE
10, 12, 15, 21, 25, 30, 40 years
STRENGTH
40%, 43%, 46%, 60%
TASTE RATING
3–4, 5 (60%)
MINIATURES
Yes

COMMENTS

A whisky of true character, Glenfarclas is acknowledged as one of the classic malts. It has a rich, sherry bouquet, a well-rounded, fruity body and a delicious, mellow finish.

VISITORS

Visitors are welcome 0930– 1700 Mon.–Fri., Apr.– Sept.; 1000– 1600 Sat., Jun.– Sept.; 1000–1600 Mon.–Fri., Oct.–Mar. or by appointment. Large parties should arrange in advance. Telephone 01807-500209 or e-mail: J&GGrant@glenfarclas. demon.co.uk

*G*lenfarclas is one of the few independently owned distilleries left in Scotland. Founded in 1836, it was bought in 1865 by J. & G. Grant (who are not related to the family of Grants at Glenfiddich) and is still in family hands. Glenfarclas bottles a wide range of single malts of varying ages and strengths. The distillery is set in an isolated spot by Ben Rinnes yet it attracts in excess of 60,000 people a year to its well-maintained visitor facilities.

Glenfiddich

Glenfiddich Distillery,
Dufftown, Keith, Banffshire

TYPE
Single malt

BOTTLING AGE
No age given

STRENGTH
40%

TASTE RATING
2

MINIATURES
Yes

COMMENTS
Glenfiddich has a light, peaty aroma with a smooth, counter-balancing sweetness. It offers an excellent introduction to malt whisky, and is ideal, too, as an aperitif.

VISITORS
Visitors are welcome 0930–1630 Mon.–Fri. all year; 0930–1630 Sat., 1200–1630 Sun., Easter–mid-Oct. Large parties should arrange in advance. Telephone 01340-820373.

Glenfiddich Distillery was started by William Grant, a former apprentice shoemaker who worked at Mortlach, another Dufftown distillery, until he gained enough knowledge and money to set up on his own in 1887. The new distillery was successful as soon as it went into production, and has remained so ever since, thanks not only to the quality and accessibility of its product but also to far-sighted marketing which has made its single malt possibly the best-known in the world. The distillery is part of the largest family-owned independent whisky company.

Glen Garioch

Glen Garioch Distillery,
Old Meldrum, Aberdeenshire

TYPE
Single malt
BOTTLING AGE
8, 15, 21, 29 years
STRENGTH
40%, 43%
TASTE RATING
3
MINIATURES
Yes
COMMENTS

Set in the small Aberdeenshire market town of Old Meldrum, Glen Garioch was reputedly founded in 1797. It has had several owners throughout its history, and was sold by the Distillers Company Ltd in 1970 to Morrison Distillers Ltd, two years after its closure because of a shortage of water. Having sunk a new well, Morrison were able to tap sufficient sources of spring water to enable normal production to continue. The company also added pioneering methods of heat and energy conservation: waste heat and carbon dioxide from the distillation and fermentation process is used to heat greenhouses which produce vegetables for the local community. The distillery has now been mothballed and its long-term future seems uncertain.

This medium-bodied whisky, with its light texture and smoky flavour, is an ideal after-dinner dram.

VISITORS

The distillery is not open to visitors.

Glengoyne

Glengoyne Distillery,
Dumgoyne, Stirlingshire

TYPE

Single malt

BOTTLING AGE

10, 12, 17 years

STRENGTH

40%, 43%

TASTE RATING

2–3

MINIATURES

Yes

COMMENTS

A light, pleasant, sweetish whisky with a fragrant aroma and no abrasive edges. Ideal as an aperitif.

VISITORS

Visitors are welcome during working hours, Mon.–Sat. Large parties (of ten and over) are requested to book ahead. Telephone 01360-550254 to arrange.

*G*lengoyne stands just north of the Highland Line (the line initiated by the Customs and Excise to differentiate area boundaries between styles of whisky) and so qualifies as a Highland distillery. It was built in 1833 at the foot of the Campsie Fells, near the fifty-foot waterfall from which it takes its supplies. It was bought by Lang Brothers in 1876 and was sympathetically restored and extended in the 1960s.

Glen Grant

Glen Grant Distillery,
Rothes, Moray

TYPE
Single malt

BOTTLING AGE
5, 10 years

STRENGTH
40%, 43%

TASTE RATING
2

MINIATURES
No

COMMENTS

The 5-year-old is light and dry, making it ideal as an aperitif, while the older version has a sweeter, fruitier, more rounded character.

VISITORS

Visitors are welcome 1000–1600 Mon.–Sat., 1130–1600 Sun., mid-Mar.–end Oct.; 1000–1700 Mon.–Sat., 1130–1700 Sun., Jun.–Sept. Telephone 01542-783318.

Opened by James and John Grant in 1840, Glen Grant enjoyed continuous expansion throughout the last century, and this has continued to the present day. The company was amalgamated with the Smiths of Glenlivet in the 1950s to form The Glenlivet and Glen Grant Distillers, which in turn merged with the Edinburgh blending firm of Hill Thomson in 1970 to form The Glenlivet Distillers. Glen Grant is now part of Seagram. The distillery's Five Years Old single malt is the best-selling malt whisky in Italy.

Glen Keith

Glen Keith Distillery,
Keith, Banffshire

TYPE

Single malt

BOTTLING AGE

10

STRENGTH

43%

TASTE RATING

2

MINIATURES

Yes

COMMENTS

A difficult-to-find, smooth and sweet-tasting Speyside single malt which is occasionally available from independent bottlers.

VISITORS

The distillery is open by appointment. Telephone 01542-783042 to arrange.

Glen Keith was built by Chivas Brothers in 1958, across the River Isla from Strathisla, another of their distilleries and one of the oldest in Scotland. As if by deliberate contrast, processes used at Glen Keith are innovative, and it was the first of the Scotch whisky distilleries to have its production processes automated. Unlike the usual practice, distillations are not bottled at fixed ages but are individually selected at what is judged to be the optimum point in the maturation process.

Glenkinchie

Glenkinchie Distillery, Pencaitland, East Lothian

TYPE
Single malt

BOTTLING AGE
10 years

STRENGTH
43%

TASTE RATING
3

MINIATURES
Yes

COMMENTS

Ideal as an aperitif, Glenkinchie, the Edinburgh malt, is the driest and smokiest of Lowland whiskies. It is a fine, pale, smooth whisky.

VISITORS

Visitors are welcome 0930–1700 Mon.–Fri all year; 0930–1700 Sat. and 1200–1700 Sun., Jun.–Oct. Telephone 01875-342004.

Glenkinchie takes its name from the burn which flows by it and the glen in which it stands. It was established in the late 1830s and has been in production since, except during the wars. The licence is held by Haig, the brand owned by United Distillers and Vintners, and most of Glenkinchie's product goes into their blends. The single malt was officially bottled by UDV in their Classic Malts series.

The Glenlivet

The Glenlivet Distillery, Ballindalloch, Banffshire

TYPE
Single malt

BOTTLING AGE
12, 18, 21 years

STRENGTH
40%, 43%

TASTE RATING
3–4

MINIATURES
Yes

COMMENTS

The Glenlivet is a subtly balanced malt. Its light, delicate bouquet has traces of fruit, and floral notes, while the complex flavours are delicately balanced between a medium sweetness and smooth dryness.

VISITORS

Visitors are welcome 1000–1600 Mon.–Sat., 1230–1600 Sun. mid-Mar.–end Oct.; 1000–1800 daily July–Aug. Telephone 01542-783220.

*T*his was one of the first distilleries licensed under the reforming 1823 Licensing Act – a fact which so incensed his still-illegal neighbours that its founder, George Smith, was obliged to carry pistols for his own protection. The whisky so grew in popularity that other distillers adopted the name, and an ensuing legal case and settlement (which endures to this day) allowed the Smiths to use the direct article in their whisky's name while others were to use it as a hyphenated suffix. In 1999, two new Glenlivet malts were launched, a 12-year-old French oak finish and the 21-year-old Archive.

CONNOISSEURS CHOICE

HIGHLAND
Single Malt Scotch Whisky

DISTILLED AT

GLENLOCHY
DISTILLERY
Proprietors: D. & J. McCallum Ltd.

DISTILLED
1977

Specially selected, produced
and bottled by
Gordon & MacPhail
Elgin · Scotland
Product of Scotland

70cl   40% vol

Glenlochy
Glenochy Distillery,
Fort William, Inverness-shire

TYPE	
Single malt	
BOTTLING AGE	
Varies	
STRENGTH	
Varies	
TASTE RATING	
2	
MINIATURES	
Yes	
COMMENTS	

*G*lenlochy Distillery was built close to Loch Lochy at the southern end of the Caledonian Canal in a pretty setting on the outskirts of Fort William. It was built in 1900 with production beginning the following year. The single malt is now something of a rarity, as almost all of the distillery's produce went into blends. The situation will not improve, as Glenlochy was closed by its parent company, United Distillers, in the 1980s and sold outside the industry in 1991.

A floral bouquet leads into a clean, dryish-tasting malt with a rather quick finish. Light-bodied and good as an aperitif.

Glenlossie

*Glenlossie-Glenlivet Distillery,
Birnie, Elgin, Moray*

TYPE

Single malt

BOTTLING AGE

10 years

STRENGTH

43%

TASTE RATING

2

MINIATURES

Yes

COMMENTS

Another whisky which is difficult to find, Glenlossie has a fresh, grassy aroma with a touch of fruitiness and a smooth, lingering flavour.

VISITORS

The distillery is not open to visitors.

SPEYSIDE
SINGLE MALT *SCOTCH WHISKY*

The three *spirit stills* at the

GLENLOSSIE

distillery have *purifiers* installed between the *lyne arm* and the *condenser*. This has a bearing on the *character* of the *single* MALT SCOTCH WHISKY produced which has a *fresh, grassy* aroma and a *smooth, lingering* flavour. Built in 1876 by *John Duff*, the *distillery* lies four miles *south* of ELGIN in *Morayshire*.

A G E D **10** Y E A R S

43% vol   70 cl

Distilled & Bottled in SCOTLAND. GLENLOSSIE DISTILLERY, Elgin, Moray, Scotland

*G*lenlossie was built not far from the River Lossie in 1876 by a former distillery manager-turned-hotel owner from Lhanbryde, near Elgin. It was expanded and improved between 1896 and 1917. In 1962, its stills were increased from four to six, while in 1992 a new mash tun was fitted. The licensee is presently Haig and the distillery is owned by United Distillers and Vintners. The single malt is still relatively rare, but became available in official bottlings in UDV's Distillery (Flora and Fauna) Malts series early in the 1990s.

Glen Mhor

*Glen Mhor Distillery,
Inverness, Inverness-shire*

TYPE	
Single malt	
BOTTLING AGE	
Varies	
STRENGTH	
Varies	
TASTE RATING	
3	
MINIATURES	
Yes	
COMMENTS	

*T*his distillery was built between 1892 and 1894 by Mackinlay and Birnie who were later to own the neighbouring Glen Albyn Distillery; John Birnie had previously managed Glen Albyn. Glen Mhor used the same water (from Loch Ness) and peat as its neighbour, but their whiskies were quite different. It was one of the first distilleries in Scotland to introduce mechanical malting in the late 1940s. It was also one of the Scottish Malt Distillers distilleries closed down by the Distillers Company Ltd in 1983, and was demolished in 1988.

Smooth and medium-bodied, Glen Mhor has a pleasant, subtle sweetness complemented by a dryish, heathery aftertaste.

Glenmorangie

*Glenmorangie Distillery,
Tain, Ross-shire*

TYPE

Single malt

BOTTLING AGE

10, 15, 18 years

STRENGTH

40%, 43%

TASTE RATING

3–4

MINIATURES

Yes

COMMENTS

A smooth and medium bodied whisky, with a delicate, slightly sweet aroma. Scotland's best-selling single malt.

VISITORS

Visitors are welcome 0900–1700 Mon.–Fri. all year; Sat. 1000–1600, Sun. 1200–1600, Jul.–Aug.; or by appointment. Telephone 01862-892477.

*D*istilling was begun here in 1843 by the Mathieson family as a sideline to farming. In 1918, The Glenmorangie Distillery Company passed into the control of its present owners, Macdonald and Muir Ltd. Water is supplied by unusually hard, mineral-rich springs in nearby Tarlogie Forest, and the lightly peated new spirit is distilled in Glenmorangie's characteristically tall, swan-necked stills, before being transferred into charred American oak barrels for the maturation process.

Glenmorangie
Port Wood Finish

Glenmorangie Distillery,
Tain, Ross-shire

TYPE
Single Malt

BOTTLING AGE
At least 12 years

STRENGTH
43%

TASTE RATING
3

MINIATURES
Yes

COMMENTS

*T*his malt is one of a series of newcomers to Glenmorangie's single malts range. In its final 'finishing' period of maturation, the whisky is transferred not into the usual charred American oak bourbon barrels, but into casks which have previously contained port. This second wood imparts its own new qualities which enhance, without overpowering, the delicate and subtle core flavours. Glenmorangie also produce two other single malts which have been aged in Madeira and sherry casks.

This whisky has a sweet aroma with minty notes and a dry, very smooth taste. The port flavours of the final maturing process come through on the lingering and quite satisfying finish.

VISITORS

Visitors are welcome 0900–1700 Mon.–Fri. all year; Sat. 1000–1600, Sun. 1200–1600, Jul.–Aug.; or by appointment. Telephone 01862-892477.

Glen Moray

*Glen Moray-Glenlivet
Distillery,
Elgin, Moray*

TYPE

Single malt

BOTTLING AGE

12, 16 years, plus a no-age-
statement bottling

STRENGTH

40%, 43%

TASTE RATING

2–3

MINIATURES

Yes

COMMENTS

A fruity, creamy and very
complex whisky. Pleasantly
dry, light and smooth, this is a
fine example of a Speyside
single malt.

VISITORS

Visitors are welcome by
appointment. Telephone 01343-
542577 to arrange.

*E*stablished during the whisky
boom years of the 1890s, the
Glen Moray-Glenlivet Distillery was
expanded in 1958. Since the 1920s it
has been owned by Macdonald &
Muir Ltd and, in addition to its
availability as a single malt, its
produce also features in many well-
known blends. Glen Moray is the
sister distillery to the better-known
Glenmorangie.

Glen Ord

*Glen Ord Distillery,
Muir of Ord, Ross-shire*

TYPE

Single malt

BOTTLING AGE

12 years

STRENGTH

40%

TASTE RATING

2–3

MINIATURES

Yes

COMMENTS

A smooth, well-rounded and slightly dry malt with a fragrant bouquet and mellow finish.

VISITORS

Visitors are welcome 0930–1700 Mon.–Fri., Mar.–Oct.; also 0930–1700 Sat. and 1230–1700 Sun., Jul.–Sept. Restricted hours Nov.–Feb. Telephone 01463-872004

*T*his distillery stands in an area which was infamous for illicit distillation even as late as a century ago. It stands on a tributary of the River Conan, the Oran Burn, whose clear waters have been used by legal and illegal whisky producers alike. Ord Distillery, as it then was, was founded in 1838 on land leased from the Mackenzies of Ord to provide a ready market for barley produced on Mackenzie farms. It was acquired by Dewar in 1923, and is now owned by United Distillers and Vintners.

The Glenrothes

*Glen Rothes Distillery,
Rothes, Moray*

TYPE

Single malt

BOTTLING AGE

Varies

STRENGTH

43%

TASTE RATING

3–4

MINIATURES

Yes

COMMENTS

A popular, full-bodied single malt with a fruity, slightly sherried aroma and a pleasingly smooth aftertaste.

VISITORS

The distillery is not open to visitors.

*T*he Glen Rothes Distillery was built in 1878 for William Grant & Sons with the backing of a group of local businessmen, including the provost of Rothes. It was bought in 1887 by the Islay Distillery Company, owners of Bunnahabhain, and then became part of the Highland Distilleries company. They still own the distillery today. Glen Rothes has been expanded twice in the last thirty years. The Glen Rothes single malt is produced and distributed by Berry Brothers & Rudd, the owners of Cutty Sark whisky, in which Glen Rothes also features.

Glen Scotia

*Glen Scotia Distillery,
Campbeltown, Argyll*

TYPE
Single malt

BOTTLING AGE
12 years

STRENGTH
40%

TASTE RATING
3

MINIATURES
Yes

COMMENTS

Glen Scotia is a rich, peaty, oily malt with a pungent aroma and a smooth, well-rounded finish.

VISITORS

Visitors are welcome by appointment. Telephone 01586-552288.

Scotia, as it was previously known, was one of thirty-two Campbeltown distilleries operating last century, partly explaining why the town has its own regional classification, even though only two distilleries remain. Glen Scotia Distillery was built in 1835 and has had many owners, the ghost of one of whom is said to haunt the place. It is currently owned by Loch Lomond Distillery Co. Ltd, the owners of Loch Lomond Distillery and the producers of Inchmurrin, Loch Lomond and Old Rhosdu single malts. Like its sister distillery, Littlemill at Bowling, Glen Scotia was mothballed for some time. However, it was brought back into production in mid-1999.

Glentauchers

*Glentauchers Distillery,
Mulben, Banffshire*

TYPE
Single malt

BOTTLING AGE
Varies

STRENGTH
40%

TASTE RATING
2

MINIATURES
Yes

COMMENTS

The sweetness of Glentauchers' aroma and taste are balanced by the light dryness of its finish. A nice pre-dinner dram, but generally available only from independent merchants.

VISITORS

The distillery has no reception centre but visitors are welcome by appointment. Telephone 01542-860272 to arrange.

*G*lentauchers was built in 1898 by James Buchanan, the entrepreneur responsible for the success of Black & White whisky, and its product went into their blends. Buchanan was a larger-than-life figure: in 1920 the then PM Lloyd George offered him the title, Lord Woolavington, in return for a healthy donation to Liberal Party funds. Buchanan was keen to take up his offer but, in keeping with his own business acumen and Lloyd George's reputation, he signed his cheque 'Woolavington'. Buchanan's distillery was largely rebuilt and modernized in 1965 but was silent for several years in the 1980s until Allied Distillers acquired it from United Distillers in 1988 and immediately reopened it.

The Glenturret

*Glenturret Distillery,
The Hosh, Crieff, Perthshire*

TYPE

Single malt

BOTTLING AGE

12, 18, 21, 25 years

STRENGTH

40%

TASTE RATING

3–4

MINIATURES

Yes

COMMENTS

*G*lenturret stands in a lovely position on the banks of the River Turret, in an area where smuggling and illicit distillation were rife in the past. It is probable that the distillery's own eighteenth-century origins lie there; some of its buildings date from that time. Glenturret was closed and partially dismantled in the 1920s until 1959, when it was largely rebuilt, anticipating the huge upswing in demand for blended whiskies in the 1960s. Today its visitor facilities are among the best of any Scots whisky distillery.

Glenturret is an award-winning, full-bodied Highland malt with a rich, nutty flavour and nicely rounded finish.

VISITORS

Visitors are welcome all year. Telephone 01764-656565.

The Glenturret Original Malt Liqueur

Glenturret Distillery,
The Hosh, Crieff, Perthshire

TYPE

Liqueur

STRENGTH

35%

TASTE RATING

3

MINIATURES

Yes

COMMENTS

A blend of herbs and The Glenturret single malt produce a smooth, delicately flavoured drink that can be enjoyed on its own or as a base for mixers.

VISITORS

Visitors are welcome all year. Telephone 01764-656565.

The Glenturret Original Malt Liqueur is produced at Scotland's oldest working distillery, officially established in 1775 but with a history predating this by some sixty years. Glenturret Distillery stands in a lovely position on the banks of the River Turret, in an area where smuggling and illicit distillation were rife in the past. Glenturret was closed from the 1920s until 1959, when it was largely rebuilt and its fortunes restored under the direction of the Fairlie family. Facilities for visitors are among the best of any distillery.

Glenugie

*Glenugie Distillery,
Peterhead, Aberdeenshire*

TYPE

Single malt

BOTTLING AGE

Varies

STRENGTH

Varies

TASTE RATING

2

MINIATURES

Yes

COMMENTS

A medium-bodied whisky with a sweetish, malty flavour and a fruity aroma. Available from independent bottlers.

*G*lenugie was the easternmost distillery in Scotland, located in Peterhead, the fishing capital of the north-east. The distillery was first established in the 1830s, and was completely rebuilt in 1875. Although enjoyable, its produce never attained the status of a classic. Glenugie Distillery was closed permanently in 1982 and sold outside the industry. Although there were never any official bottlings under the distillery's own label, supplies from the independent merchants are still available.

Grand Macnish

*Macduff International,
Glasgow*

TYPE

Blend

STRENGTH

40%, 43%

TASTE RATING

2

MINIATURES

Yes

COMMENTS

A light, very smooth blend in which the sweetness of the predominantly Highland whiskies comes through on the finish.

VISITORS

The blending and bottling plant is not open to visitors.

*G*rand MacNish is produced by Macduff International Ltd, an independent Scotch whisky company. The brand was first established by Robert McNish in 1863, the early days of whisky-blending. It is presently available as both a standard blend and a twelve-year-old, and is marketed in a unique seventeenth-century style bottle. As well as Grand MacNish, Macduff's product range includes the Islay Mist deluxe blend and Lauders, one of the oldest blends on the market.

William Grant's Family Reserve

Girvan Distillery,
Girvan, Ayrshire

TYPE

Blend

STRENGTH

40%

TASTE RATING

2

MINIATURES

Yes

COMMENTS

A traditional yet individual blend of smooth character with a light, fresh taste which incorporates elements of Glenfiddich and The Balvenie.

VISITORS

The plant is not open to visitors.

*T*he Grants of Glenfiddich, producers of the world's biggest-selling single malt whisky, are responsible for the production of two blends: William Grant's Family Reserve and Grant's 12 Years Old, the latter being a de luxe blend. The company began as malt whisky distillers in 1887 at Glenfiddich, moving into blending and exporting in 1898 after Pattison, one of the largest blenders and wholesale merchants, and Grant's biggest buyers, went bankrupt. In 1962 the company built a large complex at Girvan, housing a grain distillery, a malt distillery (Ladyburn, now dismantled), and blending facilities. Blended products are bottled at a site in Paisley.

Haig

*United Distillers and Vintners,
Banbeath, Leven, Fife*

TYPE

Blend

STRENGTH

43%

TASTE RATING

2

MINIATURES

Yes

VISITORS

A nicely balanced whisky with a fragrant aroma, Haig is smooth and easy to drink, with a long, sweet finish.

*H*aig is a family name long associated with the whisky industry, going back almost 350 years, when Robert Haig, a farmer of Stirlingshire, was rebuked by his local kirk session for distilling his whisky on a Sunday. The family had connections by marriage to the Steins, another of the big Lowland distilling families, and the Jamesons, the Dublin whiskey distillers. The Haigs were instrumental in introducing new practices and machinery (for example, the new patent still in the 1830s) to the grain distilleries which they built in Edinburgh and the east. The company was acquired by the Distillers Company in 1919 and is now owned by United Distillers and Vintners.

Heather Cream

Inver House Distillers, Moffat Distillery, Airdrie, Lanarkshire

TYPE
Cream liqueur

STRENGTH
17%

TASTE RATING
2

MINIATURES
Yes

COMMENTS
Heather Cream is a sweet blend of cream and malt whisky, and is one of the most popular of the Scotch whisky cream liqueurs available today.

VISITORS
The distillery and plant are not open to visitors.

Heather Cream was first produced by Inver House Distillers in 1980 and is the original Scottish cream liqueur. Inver House also produce Pinwinnie de luxe blend, among others. They are owners of Knockdhu (producing An Cnoc single malt) and Speyburn-Glenlivet distilleries, and have recently added to their complement of malt distilleries by buying Pulteney and Balblair from Allied Distillers and Balmanach Distillery from UDV. Heather Cream is produced at their complex at Moffat Distillery on the outskirts of Airdrie; a converted former paper mill, it is also home to a grain distillery.

Highland Park

*Highland Park Distillery,
Kirkwall, Orkney*

TYPE
Single malt

BOTTLING AGE
12 years

STRENGTH
40%

TASTE RATING
3–4

MINIATURES
Yes

COMMENTS

Highland Park is a medium-bodied single malt of character, with a heathery–smoky aroma and peaty flavour with balancing sweet tones.

VISITORS

Visitors are welcome 1000–1600 Mon.–Fri., Apr.–Oct., 1200–1600 Sat.–Sun., Jun.–Sept. Tour at 1400 Mon.–Fri., Nov.–Mar. Large groups should book in advance. Telephone 01856-874619.

*H*ighland Park's origins are linked with an illegal bothy which previously occupied the site. Its owner was one of whisky's most colourful characters, Magnus Eunson. A United Presbyterian church elder by day and smuggler by night, his piety did not prevent his using the church pulpit as a handy hiding place for his illicit distillations. The distillery was founded in 1798 and passed to the Grant family in 1895. Highland Distilleries purchased it in 1937. The different nature of Orcadian peat is said to be a factor in the quite distinctive qualities of the islands' whiskies. Highland Park is the more widely available of the islands' two malts.

Immortal Memory

*Gordon and MacPhail,
Elgin, Moray*

TYPE	Blend
BOTTLING AGE	8 years
STRENGTH	40%
TASTE RATING	2
MINIATURES	Yes

COMMENTS

A blend which is floral on the nose – perhaps with a hint of parma violets – with a nutty flavour and a warming finish.

VISITORS

Gordon and MacPhail's shop, South St, Elgin is open 0900–1715 Mon.–Wed. (0900–1300 Wed. in winter), 0830–1715 Thu.–Fri., 0900–1700 Sat.

*G*ordon and MacPhail started in business in 1895 as a licensed grocers and wine and spirit merchant, as had done so many of the foremost names among the Scotch whisky blending industry. Unlike the others, however, Gordon and MacPhail have retained all the original aspects of their business as well as extending into vatting, blending and bottling. This blend was declared 'Best Blended Whisky in the World' at the 1991 International Wine and Spirit Competition.

Imperial

Imperial Distillery,
Carron, Moray

TYPE

Single malt

BOTTLING AGE

Varies

STRENGTH

Varies

TASTE RATING

4

MINIATURES

Yes

COMMENTS

A full-bodied malt with bags of character, Imperial contrives to balance a rich sweetness with a lingering smokiness. Available from independent merchants.

VISITORS

The distillery has no reception centre but visitors are welcome by appointment. Telephone 01340-810276 to arrange.

*T*he patriotically named Imperial Distillery was first established in 1897, the year of Queen Victoria's Diamond Jubilee. Its founder was Thomas Mackenzie, who was already the owner of Dailuaine and Talisker distilleries. All three were brought together under the name of Dailuaine-Talisker Distilleries Ltd. Imperial Distillery was modernized in the mid 1950s. Production was halted temporarily in the 1980s, but was restarted again after Imperial's purchase by Allied Distillers in 1988, and its production now goes into their blends.

Inchgower

*Inchgower Distillery,
Buckie, Banffshire*

TYPE

Single malt

BOTTLING AGE

14 years

STRENGTH

43%

TASTE RATING

2–3

MINIATURES

Yes

COMMENTS

A robust, distinctly heavy-bodied malt with a combination of nutty, fruity and spicy aromas, and a hint of sweetness in its tones.

VISITORS

The distillery is not open to visitors.

*I*nchgower Distillery was moved from Tochineal by its founder, Alexander Wilson, to its present site at Rathaven near Buckie, to take advantage of the ready supply of water from the Letter Burn and the Springs of Aultmoor. When the original firm went out of business, the distillery passed to Buckie Town Council who sold it to Arthur Bell & Sons for £1000 in 1938. Most of the whisky goes into Bell's blends and the distillery is now owned by United Distillers and Vintners. The single malt is still relatively rare, only becoming available in official bottlings in the Distillery (Flora and Fauna) Malts series early in the 1990s.

Inchmurrin

Loch Lomond Distillery,
Alexandria, Dunbartonshire

TYPE

Single malt

BOTTLING AGE

10 years

STRENGTH

40%

TASTE RATING

2

MINIATURES

Yes

COMMENTS

A clean, light, pre-dinner malt with a fresh, floral note. A Highland malt with a Lowland character.

VISITORS

The distillery is not open to visitors.

Loch Lomond distillery was first established in the early 19th century but has only been operating from its present site since 1966. It is the only distillery in Scotland that produces both malt and grain whisky on the same site. The malt plant has three sets of stills, capable of producing three different styles of whisky at the same time. The malt distillery currently produces seven different malts, most of which are for blends.

Invergordon

Invergordon Distillery,
Invergordon, Ross-shire

TYPE

Grain

BOTTLING AGE

10 years

STRENGTH

40%

TASTE RATING

1

MINIATURES

Yes

COMMENTS

A light, clean, smooth whisky with a gentle, slightly vanilla-like taste.

VISITORS

The distillery is not open to visitors.

*B*uilt in the late 1950s to provide work in an area of high unemployment, Invergordon grain distillery is now one of the biggest distilleries in Europe. As with certain other distilleries in the area, a provost of Inverness had a hand in its establishment. Along with the seven former Invergordon Distillers' malt distilleries, this giant grain complex was acquired in 1993 by Whyte & Mackay. Ben Wyvis malt distillery was added on the same site but is now closed.

Inverleven

Inverleven Distillery,
Dumbarton, Dunbartonshire

TYPE
Single malt

BOTTLING AGE
Varies

STRENGTH
Varies

TASTE RATING
2

MINIATURES
Yes

COMMENTS
A relatively smooth Lowland malt, with a nice balance of dry and sweet flavours. Available from independent whisky merchants only.

VISITORS
The distillery is not suitable for visitors.

*B*uilt in 1938, Inverleven is part of a modern-looking, multi-storey red-brick plant, which includes Dumbarton grain distillery, on the banks of the Leven in Dumbarton. It stands on the Highland Line (the line initiated by the Customs and Excise to differentiate area boundaries between styles of whisky), and is classified as a Lowland distillery. It is owned by Allied Distillers and almost all of its output goes into their blends, which include the popular Ballantine's, Teacher's and Long John blends.

ISLAY MIST

75cl 40% Vol

THE GREAT SEAL OF ISLAY

Deluxe

BLENDED SCOTCH WHISKY

DISTILLED, BLENDED AND BOTTLED IN SCOTLAND
MACDUFF INTERNATIONAL LIMITED

Islay Mist

MacDuff International,
Glasgow

TYPE	
De luxe	
BOTTLING AGE	
8, 12, 17 years	
STRENGTH	
40%, 43%	
TASTE RATING	
3	
MINIATURES	
Yes	
COMMENTS	

*T*he blenders of Islay Mist, MacDuff International, are an independent Scotch whisky company. This mellow Islay de luxe blend made its first appearance in 1928 to mark the twenty-first birthday of Lord Margadale. As well as Islay Mist, their product range includes Lauder's, one of the oldest blends in the Scotch whisky market, as well as Grand MacNish and Strathbeag blends.

This de luxe blend instantly betrays its origins, though as the name suggests, it is mellower in taste than its main component, Laphroaig. Islay Mist is matured in oak casks and is ideal as an introduction for those wishing to sample the delights of the Islay whiskies.

VISITORS

The blending and bottling plant is not open to visitors.

Isle of Jura

*Isle of Jura Distillery,
Craighouse, Jura, Argyll*

TYPE
Single malt

BOTTLING AGE
10 years

STRENGTH
40%, 43%

TASTE RATING
3

MINIATURES
Yes

COMMENTS
Reminiscent of a Highland malt, though with a light, clean, fragrant palate of its own, this Island malt is ideal as an aperitif.

VISITORS
Visitors are welcome by appointment. Telephone 01496-820240 to arrange.

*T*he distillery is one of the main employers on this island of around 200 inhabitants. It was first built overlooking the Sound of Jura in 1810, next to a cave where illicit distillation may have been carried on for as long as three centuries. The distillery's machinery and buildings were owned by different individuals, and a dispute between the two led to its closure for over fifty years in 1913. It was effectively redesigned and rebuilt before its reopening in the 1960s. The present owners are JBB (Greater Europe) who evolved from Whyte & Mackay who acquired it, and six other malt distilleries, after their purchase of Invergordon Distillers in 1993.

J & B Rare

Justerini and Brooks,
London

TYPE
Blend

STRENGTH
40%, 43%

TASTE RATING
2

MINIATURES
Yes

COMMENTS
J & B Rare is a smooth, sweet-tasting whisky with a light, fresh character. It is the second-best selling Scotch whisky in the world.

*J*usterini and Brooks' principal founder, Giacomo Justerini, was a wine merchant from Bologna who was infatuated by an Italian opera singer, whom he followed to London in the mid-eighteenth century. There he set up the wine merchants, Justerini & Brooks. In 1962 the company amalgamated with four others to form International Distillers and Vintners Ltd (IDV). Grand Metropolitan bought IDV, then part of Watney Mann & Truman, in 1972. As well as the very popular J & B Rare, the number two whisky worldwide, the company also produces J & B Reserve, a more mature fifteen-year-old blend, J & B Jet, a twelve-year-old de luxe whisky, and J & B Ultima, a fine blend containing no less than 128 whiskies which was launched in 1994.

J & B Jet

Justerini & Brooks,
London

TYPE

Blend

STRENGTH

43%

TASTE RATING

3

MINIATURES

No

COMMENTS

Jet has has fresh, fragrant aroma which leads into a rich, mellow taste with unexpected sweet notes.

J usterini & Brooks' principal founder, Giacomo Justerini, was a wine merchant from Bologna who was infatuated by an Italian opera singer, whom he followed to London in the mid-eighteenth century. He set up the wine merchants, Justerini and Brooks in the capital in 1749 and began selling Scotch thirty years later. In 1962 the company built on previous amalgamations by combining with W. & A. Gilbey to form International Distillers and Vintners Ltd (IDV). Grand Metropolitan bought IDV, then part of Watney Mann & Truman, in 1972. Jet took J&B twelve years to develop as a major product in the premium Scotch market. A high proportion of Speyside malts is used in its blend of twelve- and fifteen-year-old whiskies.

Johnnie Walker
Black Label

United Distillers and Vintners, Kilmarnock, Ayrshire

TYPE
De luxe

BOTTLING AGE
12 years

STRENGTH
40%

TASTE RATING
2–3

MINIATURES
Yes

COMMENTS
The best-selling de luxe Scotch whisky in the world, it has a special quality of smoothness and a depth of taste and character which linger on the palate.

*I*n common with other entrepreneurs who became the major operators in the whisky-blending industry, the original Johnnie Walker began as a licensed grocer in Kilmarnock in 1820. It was his grandsons who created the Black Label and Red Label blends in the early 1900s. His son, Alexander Walker, bought Cardow Distillery in 1893, thus ensuring a regular supply of malt for their blends. In 1925 the company joined the Distillers Company Ltd who bought the Talisker and Dailuaine distilleries and licensed the former to Walker. Johnnie Walker Black Label is now owned by United Distillers and Vintners.

Johnnie Walker *Blue Label*

United Distillers and Vintners, Kilmarnock, Ayrshire

TYPE
Blend

STRENGTH
43%

STRENGTH
2–3

MINIATURES
No

COMMENTS
Blue Label is among the most exclusive of blended whiskies, with a subtle and complex character and a rich, pleasing flavour.

*I*ntroduced to the UK market in 1992 under its new name, Blue Label is the latest and most up-market addition to the family of Johnnie Walker 'coloured label' whiskies. Most of the product is intended to go for export, particularly to Japanese markets. The Johnnie Walker company began as a family-run licensed grocers in Kilmarnock in 1820 and by the end of the century had become one of the major players in the Scotch industry. It was a Walker's employee, James Stevenson, who was instrumental in persuading the government to introduce a minimum period of maturation in bond for whisky, in the process raising quality standards and doing the industry a major service. Johnnie Walker is now one of United Distillers and Vintners' major blending names.

Johnnie Walker Red Label

United Distillers and Vintners, Kilmarnock, Ayrshire

TYPE

Blend

STRENGTH

43%

TASTE RATING

2

MINIATURES

Yes

COMMENTS

A smooth blend with sweet and dry notes of maltiness and peatiness. Red Label is the world's biggest-selling blended whisky.

*I*n common with other entrepreneurs who became the major operators in the whisky-blending industry, the original Johnnie Walker began as a licensed grocer in Kilmarnock in 1820. It was his grandsons who created the Black Label and Red Label blends in the early 1900s. His son, Alexander Walker, bought Cardow Distillery in 1893, thus ensuring a regular supply of malt for their blends. In 1925 the company joined the Distillers Company Ltd who bought the Talisker and Dailuaine distilleries and licensed the former to Walker. Johnnie Walker Red Label is now owned by United Distillers and Vintners.

Knockando

Knockando Distillery,
Knockando, Aberlour,
Banffshire

TYPE
Single malt

BOTTLING AGE
Bottled when ready, rather than at a set age; always at least twelve years.

STRENGTH
40%, 43%

TASTE RATING
3–4

MINIATURES
Yes

COMMENTS
Knockando is a light, easy-to-drink single malt, with pleasantly smooth, nutty hints.

VISITORS
Visitors are welcome by appointment. Telephone 01340-6205 to arrange.

*B*uilt during the 1890s whisky boom, Knockando is today owned by International Distillers and Vintners. The distillery's name is said to mean 'small black hill', and Knockando itself is set on a hill overlooking the Spey. Knockando single malt is bottled only when it is considered to have reached its peak rather than at a pre-determined age – generally, this is between twelve and fifteen years. The label lists the year of distillation – the 'season' – and the year of bottling. Such season dating recalls the time when Scottish distilleries only distilled during the winter season after the barley harvest.

Lagavulin

Lagavulin Distillery,
Port Ellen, Islay, Argyll

TYPE

Single malt

BOTTLING AGE

16 years

STRENGTH

43%

TASTE RATING

5

MINIATURES

Yes

COMMENTS

A distinctively Islay malt, powerful and demanding, with a dominant aroma and a dry, peaty–smoky flavour complemented by a trace of sweetness.

VISITORS

Visitors are welcome all year round Mon.–Fri. by appointment. Telephone 01496-302400 to arrange.

Distilling was carried on in this area from the 1740s, when moonshiners made and smuggled illicit whisky to the mainland. Lagavulin's own history is entangled with these times, although the distillery dates officially from the 1810s. Peter Mackie, the main driving force behind the success of White Horse, started out on his distilling career at Lagavulin, and its produce was later to feature strongly in his blend. Lagavulin went into partnership with Mackie's company, subsequently the White Horse Company, and the whisky is still used in White Horse blends today. The distillery is owned by United Distillers and Vintners.

Laphroaig

Laphroaig Distillery,
Port Ellen, Islay, Argyll

TYPE

Single malt

BOTTLING AGE

10, 15 years

STRENGTH

40%, 43%, up to 45.1%

TASTE RATING

5

MINIATURES

Yes

COMMENTS

A robust, full-bodied, classic Islay malt with a trace of seaweed in its strongly peaty flavour.

VISITORS

Visitors are welcome by appointment, Sept.–end June. Telephone 01496-302418 to arrange.

LAPHROAIG®

SINGLE ISLAY MALT
SCOTCH WHISKY

10 *Years Old*

The most richly flavoured of
all Scotch whiskies

ESTABLISHED
1815

DISTILLED AND BOTTLED IN SCOTLAND BY

D. JOHNSTON & CO., (LAPHROAIG), LAPHROAIG DISTILLERY, ISLE OF ISLAY,

40%vol   IMPORTADOR WENCESLAO PAZ MARTINEZ
DOMICILIO C HADDU S/N R.S. NUM 40.1.125 ML   70cl

Laphroaig Distillery is set on a bay on Islay's southern shore, and dates back to 1815. It is a traditional distillery and one of the few still to have a hand-turned malting floor, ensuring the traditional taste. It is owned by Allied Distillers, who consider the single malt, a top-five seller in the UK malts list and one of the top ten around the world, to be the star performer across their entire portfolio. Laphroaig is also one of the components in their Long John, Ballantine's and Teacher's blends, as well as in the quality Black Bottle blend, which Allied sold in 1995 to Matthew Gloag & Son, blenders of The Famous Grouse.

Lauder's Scotch

Macduff International,
Glasgow

TYPE

Blend

STRENGTH

40% and 43%

TASTE RATING

2

MINIATURES

Yes

COMMENTS

A smooth, nicely rounded and easy-to-drink blend.

VISITORS

The blending and bottling plant is not open to visitors.

*T*he blenders of Lauders, Macduff International, are an independent Scotch whisky company. Lauders has been in continuous production since 1836, making it one of the oldest brands available on the market. Throughout its long history, Lauders has won several gold medals in competition both at thome and overseas. As well as Lauders, Macduff International's product range includes the Islay Mist de luxe, as well as the Grand MacNish blend.

Ledaig

*Tobermory Distillery,
Tobermory, Mull, Argyll*

TYPE	
Single malt	
BOTTLING AGE	
15, 20 years	
STRENGTH	
43%	
TASTE RATING	
5	
MINIATURES	
No	

LEDAIG

SINGLE MALT
SCOTCH WHISKY
FROM
THE ISLE OF MULL

Aged *20* years

*This rare old single malt Scotch whisky
was distilled at the Ledaig Distillery
on the Isle of Mull by
Ledaig Distillers (Tobermory) Ltd.*

PRODUCE OF SCOTLAND

70cl ℮   43% Vol

COMMENTS

A full-bodied single malt, Ledaig has strongly peaty flavours.

VISITORS

The Visitor Centre and Distillery Shop are open Mon.–Fri., Easter–30 Sept. Tours can be arranged at other times in the year. Telephone 01688-302645.

Set in a wooded site by the sea, Mull's only distillery has enjoyed mixed fortunes since it was first established in 1823. Tobermory has been closed several times during its existence, most recently in the 1980s when it was mothballed. Having reopened in 1990, Tobermory is now back in production, under the control of Burn Stewart Distillers, and it remains one of the few family-owned independent whisky distilleries. The distillery was previously known as Ledaig, changing its name in the 1970s. A single malt is also available under the distillery's new name of Tobermory.

SPEYSIDE
SINGLE MALT
SCOTCH WHISKY

LINKWOOD

distillery stands on the *River Lossie,*
close to *ELGIN* in *Speyside.* The *distillery*
has retained its *traditional atmosphere*
since its *establishment* in 1821.
Great care has always
been taken to *safeguard* the
character of the *whisky* which has
remained the same through the
years. Linkwood is one of the
FINEST Single Malt Scotch Whiskies
available - *full bodied* with a *hint* of
sweetness and a *slightly smoky* aroma.

YEARS **12** OLD

43% vol   Distilled & Bottled in *SCOTLAND.*
LINKWOOD DISTILLERY
Elgin, Moray, Scotland   70cl

Linkwood

Linwood Distillery,
Elgin, Moray

TYPE
Single malt

BOTTLING AGE
12 years

STRENGTH
43%

TASTE RATING
4–5

MINIATURES
Yes

COMMENTS
Linkwood is widely acclaimed as one of the best Speyside malts, having the area's characteristics in a fine balance: smoky, and with a fruity sweetness underlying its malty tones.

VISITORS
The distillery is not open to visitors.

*T*his is one of the most traditional of distilleries despite extensive rebuilding work carried out three times since its establishment in the 1820s: it is said that equipment was never replaced until absolutely necessary, and even a spider's web was not removed in case the change of environment would affect the whisky. Built by a former provost of Elgin, Linkwood has an attractive wooded setting by Linkwood Burn outside the town. The distillery is owned by United Distillers and Vintners.

Littlemill

Littlemill Distillery,
Bowling, Dunbartonshire

SINGLE LOWLAND MALT
SCOTCH WHISKY

DISTILLED AND BOTTLED IN SCOTLAND BY

LITTLEMILL DISTILLERY CO. LTD.

BOWLING, DUNBARTONSHIRE, SCOTLAND

70cl ℮   40%vol

TYPE

Single malt

BOTTLING AGE

8 years

STRENGTH

40%

TASTE RATING

2–3

MINIATURES

Yes

COMMENTS

A light Lowland malt with a smooth, sweet flavour. Good as an aperitif.

VISITORS

The distillery is not open to the public.

Littlemill began life as a brewery centuries before distilling was started, with its ale apparently crossing the Clyde to supply the monks of Paisley Abbey. It was established as a distillery in the late eighteenth century and is one of the oldest in Scotland. Its water comes from the Kilpatrick Hills, to the north of the Highland Line (the line initiated by the Customs and Excise to differentiate the area boundaries between different styles of whisky), although Littlemill is a Lowland distillery and whisky. Owned until 1994 by Gibson International, it is now, with its sister distillery of Glen Scotia, under the control of the Loch Lomond Distillery Co., the producers of Inchmurrin single malt. Littlemill is presently mothballed.

The Loch Fyne

Loch Fyne Whiskies,
Inveraray, Argyll

TYPE

Blend

STRENGTH

40%

TASTE RATING

2–3

MINIATURES

Yes

COMMENTS

A malt drinker's blend, full flavoured, with a raisiny, sweet spiced nose, mellow smoothness of taste and a warmng finish. A very easy-to-drink whisky.

VISITORS

The shop is open all year, 1000–1730 (except Sun., Nov.–Mar.). Telephone 01499-302219 for mail-order information.

*L*och Fyne Whiskies is an independent specialist shop devoted to selling only whisky and whisky-related products. First registered in 1884, the current Loch Fyne blend was created by Ronnie Martin, a former production director of DCL/United Distillers. His mastery of blending was recognised when in 1996, The Loch Fyne won the bronze award in the influential International Wine & Spirit Competition. Produced in small quantities, The Loch Fyne is available only in Argyll or by mail-order. (Postal customers also receive a copy of the company's informed, witty and enthusiastic biannual newsletter, *Scotch Whisky Review*.)

Loch Ranza

Isle of Arran Distillers,
Lochranza, Isle of Arran

TYPE

Blend

STRENGTH

40%

TASTE RATING

2

MINIATURES

Yes

COMMENTS

In its distinctive blue bottle, Loch Ranza is a very smooth and relatively sweet blend, making it an ideal pre-dinner dram.

VISITORS

The distillery and visitor centre is open daily, Mar.–Oct.

*I*sle of Arran Distillers is a dynamic new force in the Scotch whisky market and are one of the few independent distillers in the country. In 1994, they opened Scotland's newest malt whisky distillery at Lochranza in which traditional methods of production are carried out within a state-of-the-art building. The new spirit was laid down in 1995 and four years later, ahead of company expectations, a limited stock of Arran malt was launched after it was discovered that the whisky had matured remarkably quickly. This malt is a major component in Loch Ranza.

HIGHLAND MALT SCOTCH WHISKY
FROM
**LOCHSIDE
DISTILLERY**
Proprietors Macnab Distilleries Ltd.
40%vol DISTILLED **1981** ~ BOTTLED 1998 70cl
SPECIALLY SELECTED, PRODUCED & BOTTLED BY GORDON & MACPHAIL, ELGIN, SCOTLAND

Lochside

*Lochside Distillery,
Montrose, Angus*

TYPE

Single malt

BOTTLING AGE

10 years

STRENGTH

40%

TASTE RATING

2

MINIATURES

No

COMMENTS

*E*stablished as recently as 1957, Lochside has been one of the shorter-lived Scotch whisky distilleries. It was built on the site of an eighteenth-century brewery and originally comprised two distilleries, one grain and one malt, as well as a blending plant. The distillery closed its grain-distilling and blending facilities in the late 1970s and continued in malt production only until 1992, when it was shut down completely by its Spanish owners.

A light-to-medium-bodied single malt with a sweet, fruity aroma and drier, smooth flavour. It is increasingly difficult to find under the distillery label, but supplies will continue to be available from independent merchants.

Long John

Allied Distillers,
Dumbarton, Dumbartonshire

TYPE

Blend

STRENGTH

40%, 43%

TASTE RATING

2–3

MINIATURES

Yes

COMMENTS

A medium-bodied blend with a very slight peaty tang to its pleasant, nicely rounded flavour.

VISITORS

Visitors are welcome by appointment.

*T*he original company was founded by 'Long' John Macdonald, a statuesque man who built Ben Nevis Distillery at Fort William in 1825. The distillery had grain and malt stills, and its produce changed from a malt to a blend around the turn of the century. The Long John company name and the distillery went separate ways, and the company was bought by Chaplin, a London wine and spirit merchant in 1911. They in turn were acquired by the spirit merchants Seager, Evans in 1936. The company changed its name to Long John International in 1971 and, after several acquisitions, it is now operated by Allied Distillers.

172

Longmorn

Longmorn Distillery,
Elgin, Moray

TYPE	
Single malt	
BOTTLING AGE	
15 years	
STRENGTH	
45%	
TASTE RATING	
3–4	
MINIATURES	
Yes	

COMMENTS

Another classic Speyside malt of great character, Longmorn is a full-bodied whisky with a clean, fragrant aroma and a nutty, sweet taste.

VISITORS

The distillery is not open to visitors.

*T*he distillery was built by John Duff in 1894 and stands on the road between Elgin and Rothes. Nearby is an old water wheel dating from the seventeenth century, although the distillery draws its water from a local spring. Longmorn, along with its sister distillery of Benriach, merged with The Glenlivet and Glen Grant Distilleries and Hill Thomson to form The Glenlivet Distillers. The distillery at that time was known as Longmorn-Glenlivet, but has now dropped its hyphenated suffix. The company was purchased by Seagram in 1976.

Longrow

Springbank Distillery,
Campbeltown, Argyll

TYPE

Single malt

BOTTLING AGE

10, 25 years

STRENGTH

46%

TASTE RATING

5

MINIATURES

Yes

COMMENTS

Longrow is a pungent malt whose production process, using only peat-dried barley, lends it a distinctive, peaty taste with an almost medicinal aroma, yet a complementary trace of sweetness. It is also now available in a sherrywood matured version.

VISITORS

Springbank Distillery is open to visitors strictly by appointment. Telephone 01586-552085 to arrange.

Springbank Distillery produces Longrow as its second malt. It is called after another Campbeltown distillery of that name, which was closed in the late 1800s. The Longrow malt is so strongly peated that it has often been likened to an Islay malt. Springbank is a one-off among Scots distilleries for several reasons: it is the only distillery-label malt which follows traditional techniques of not chill-filtering; it is the only distillery to carry out all production techniques, from floor malting to bottling; it is the only distillery in Campbeltown not to have closed; and it has been owned by the same family for close on two centuries.

The Macallan

Macallan Distillery,
Craigellachie, Banffshire

TYPE
Single malt
BOTTLING AGE
7, 10, 12, 18, 25 years
STRENGTH
40%, 43%, 57%
TASTE RATING
3–4
MINIATURES
Yes
COMMENTS

Its rich, sherried aroma with a hint of fruit and spices, its smooth, slightly sweet flavour and its delightfully mellow aftertaste make the Macallan one of the most popular of malts

VISITORS

Visitors are welcome by appointment on weekdays. Telephone 01340-871471.

*T*he Macallan's distinctive richness of taste and colour derives in part from its ageing in sweet sherry casks, a traditional practice which this distillery is the only one to maintain through all its range. The distillery itself originated on a farm set above a ford over the River Spey which was used by drovers travelling south. Distilling was probably under way on this site in the 1700s with the first licensed distilling taking place around 1824. It was bought and extended in 1892 by Richard Kemp, whose descendants owned the company until it was acquired by Highland Distilleries in 1996. The Macallan is regularly rated among Scotland's top three single malts and earns many accolades.

Millburn

*Millburn Distillery,
Inverness, Inverness-shire*

TYPE
Single malt

BOTTLING AGE
Varies

STRENGTH
Varies

TASTE RATING
3–4

MINIATURES
Yes

COMMENTS

A rich Highland malt of medium-to-full body with a certain fruitiness in the palate and a balancing dry finish. Available from independent merchants.

M illburn was one of three Inverness distilleries (the others being Glen Albyn and Glen Mhor), none of which is still in existence, Millburn itself having been closed in 1985 and later sold off by its owners, United Distillers. It was also one of the older Highland distilleries, having been established around 1825, although distilling was said to have been carried out on the site as early as 1807. All its produce was traditionally used for blending, so it is difficult to find as a single and its malt will, of course, become rarer in future.

10
YEARS OLD
MILTONDUFF

70cl   SINGLE SPEYSIDE   40%vol
MALT

TRADEMARK OF PROPRIETORS
GEORGE BALLANTINE & SON
SPECIALLY SELECTED, PRODUCED AND BOTTLED BY
AND UNDER THE RESPONSIBILITY OF
GORDON & MACPHAIL, ELGIN, SCOTLAND.
REGISTERED BOTTLER.
PRODUCT OF SCOTLAND

Miltonduff

Miltonduff-Glenlivet
Distillery, Elgin, Moray

TYPE
Single malt

BOTTLING AGE
10 years

STRENGTH
40%

TASTE RATING
2–3

MINIATURES
No

COMMENTS
A nice Speyside malt, medium-bodied and smooth, with a floral note.

VISITORS
Visitors are welcome by appointment. Telephone 01343-547433 to arrange.

Miltonduff-Glenlivet Distillery stands just to the south of Elgin near Pluscarden Abbey; the distillery's old mashhouse was said to have been built on the site of the abbey's brewery. The distillery itself was founded in 1824, and draws its water from the nearby Black Burn which flows down peaty Black Hill. Miltonduff was one of the original Hiram Walker distilleries acquired in 1937 and today is operated by Allied Distillers who use it in their blends, notably Ballantine's. The single malt is only available from independent bottlers.

Mitchell's

J. & A. Mitchell & Co.,
Campbeltown, Argyll

TYPE

Blend

STRENGTH

43%

TASTE RATING

2–3

MINIATURES

No

COMMENTS

Mitchell's is a full-bodied premium blend with a rich, sweet flavour that points to its high malt content.

itchell's 12-Year-Old is one of two blended whiskies produced at Springbank Distillery in Campbeltown. Springbank is the oldest distillery in Scotland still in the ownership of its founders. It was built in 1828 on the site of an earlier illicit distillery run by Archibald Mitchell, the great great grandfather of the current owners. Springbank is unusual in other ways: it has never been silent at any time in its long career; it is one of the few distilleries that does not colour or chill-filter its distillery malts and actually carries out the full production process from floor malting to bottling on the premises.

SPEYSIDE
SINGLE MALT
SCOTCH WHISKY

MORTLACH

was the first of seven *distilleries* in *Dufftown*. In the *C19th farm animals* kept in adjoining byres were fed on *barley* left over from processing. Today *water* from springs in the *CONVAL HILLS* is used to produce this delightful smooth, fruity single *MALT SCOTCH WHISKY*.

AGED **16** YEARS

Distilled & Bottled in SCOTLAND.
MORTLACH DISTILLERY,
Dufftown, Keith, Banffshire, Scotland

43% vol   70 cl

Mortlach

Mortlach Distillery,
Dufftown, Keith, Banffshire

TYPE	
Single malt	
BOTTLING AGE	
16 years	
STRENGTH	
43%	
TASTE RATING	
4	
MINIATURES	
Yes	
COMMENTS	

A Speyside malt of mellow, fruity flavour with a definite peatiness and a dryness in the finish.

VISITORS

The distillery is not open to visitors.

Another of Dufftown's distilleries, this time standing in a little valley outside the town, by the River Dullan. The distillery draws its water not from the river but from springs in the local Conval Hills. Founded in 1823, it was, in fact, the first of the distilleries to be built in the capital of Speyside whisky-making, and it enjoyed a monopoly in the town until 1887. The distillery has been modernized twice this century and is now owned by United Distillers and Vintners, who did not officially bottle its malt until it featured in the Distillery (Flora and Fauna) Malts series in the 1990s.

North Port

North Port Distillery,
Brechin, Angus

TYPE

Single malt

BOTTLING AGE

Varies

STRENGTH

Varies

TASTE RATING

2

MINIATURES

Yes

COMMENTS

Available from independent bottling merchants, North Port is a light-bodied, dry, fairly astringent whisky, best drunk as an aperitif.

*T*he older of the two distilleries in Brechin (Glencadam being the other), North Port was founded in 1820 by David Guthrie, a prominent Brechin businessman and local politician and managed by his sons from 1823; two brothers in the Guthrie family had interests in the whisky industry while a third, Thomas, was active in the temperance movement. The distillery, latterly owned by the Distillers Company Ltd, was closed down in 1983 and sold in 1990.

Oban

Oban Distillery,
Oban, Argyll

TYPE
Single malt

BOTTLING AGE
14 years

STRENGTH
43%

TASTE RATING
2–3

MINIATURES
Yes

COMMENTS

An intriguing, complex malt with a full Island character which is balanced by a soft Highland finish.

VISITORS

Visitors are welcome 0930–1700 Mon.–Fri. all year and 0930–2030 Jul.–Sept.; also 0930–1700 Sat., Jul.–Sept. Telephone 01631-572004.

*F*irst built as a brewery in 1794, Oban Distillery was part of the grand plan of the Stevensons, a family of energetic entrepreneurs and the founders of modern Oban at that time. The distillery, a grey building standing on the harbour front, draws its water from the Ardconnel area of peaty hills a mile from the town. It is licensed to John Hopkins, now owned by United Distillers and Vintners, who currently feature the single in their Classic Malts series.

Old Fettercairn

Fettercairn Distillery,
Fettercairn, Laurencekirk
Kincardineshire

TYPE

Single malt

BOTTLING AGE

10 years

STRENGTH

40%

TASTE RATING

3–4

MINIATURES

Yes

COMMENTS

A smooth single malt with a full, malty taste and a satisfyingly dry counterbalance.

VISITORS

Visitors are welcome at the distillery's visitor centre 1000–1630 Mon.–Sat., May–Sept. Telephone 01561-340205 to arrange group bookings.

*F*irst established at its present location in 1824 by Sir Alexander Ramsay, Fettercairn is one of the country's oldest distilleries. Despite its age, it proved receptive to modern production methods when it became the first distillery in the country to use oil for heating its stills. It was once owned by John Gladstone, the father of the great Victorian prime minister W. E. Gladstone. Fettercairn is situated on the fringes of the Grampian Mountains, from which it takes its spring-water supplies. The distillery, which was extended in 1966, is presently owned by Invergordon Distillers, a subsidiary of JBB (Greater Europe).

was interred at

DISTILLED AND BOTTLED IN SCOTLAND

Grand
Old Parr®

Aged 12 *Years*
De Luxe
Scotch Whisky

MACDONALD GREENLEES, DISTILLERS
EDINBURGH EH12 6JW SCOTLAND

43% vol   1 Litre

LAO N° 666051

Thomas Parr. Aged 152 years

Westminster Abbey A.D. 1635

Old Parr

United Distillers and Vintners,
Banbeath, Leven, Fife

TYPE
De luxe
BOTTLING AGE
12 years
STRENGTH
43%
TASTE RATING
2
MINIATURES
No
COMMENTS

A blend of fine whiskies, with a smooth and mellow taste and exceptional depth of flavour.

The firm which produced Old Parr, Macdonald Greenlees, is now owned by United Distillers. The brand was first produced in the early twentieth century by the Greenlees brothers from Glasgow, and was aimed specifically at the southern English market. After the First World War, the company amalgamated with Alexander & Macdonald of Leith and William Williams of Aberdeen, owners of Glendullan Distillery. The whole company joined the Distillers Company Ltd in 1925. Old Parr is a major export blend in Central and South American, Japan and the Far Eastern markets.

Old Pulteney

Pulteney Distillery,
Wick, Caithness

TYPE

Single malt

BOTTLING AGE

12 years

STRENGTH

40%, Cask strength

TASTE RATING

3–4

MINIATURES

Yes

COMMENTS

Reputedly one of the fastest-maturing whiskies, Old Pulteney is a distinctive malt with a pungent aroma and salty tang underlain by peaty notes, perhaps due to the exposed coastal position of the distillery.

VISITORS

Visitors are welcome by prior arrangement.

*P*ulteney Distillery was established in 1826 in a new district of Wick which had been built to accommodate workers from the local herring industry, and in such a situation it had a ready market. It was closed during the slump of the 1920s and was not reopened until 1951, being sold to James & George Stodart Ltd of Dumbarton, a Hiram Walker subsidiary, four years later. In June 1995 the distillery was sold by Allied Distillers to Inver House Distillers, giving them a complement of five malt distilleries, the others being Balmenach, Knockdhu, Speyburn-Glenlivet and, most recently, Balblair. The most northerly distillery on the Scottish mainland, Pultney is situated near the ruins of the fourteenth-century Castle Oliphant, known as the Auld Man o' Wick.

The Original Mackinlay

Invergordon Distillers, Leith, Edinburgh

TYPE	
Blend	
STRENGTH	
40%	
TASTE RATING	
2	
MINIATURES	
Yes	

COMMENTS

A well-balanced and nicely aged whisky with a smooth, malty aroma and a relatively full, lingering and slightly sweet flavour.

VISITORS

The blending and bottling plant is not open to visitors.

*T*he success of the Mackinlay firm began under James, son of Charles Mackinlay, founder of the Leith company in 1824. The original Mackinlays blend appeared in 1850, and James was responsible for its success in the lucrative markets of southern England, gaining contracts to supply whisky to the House of Commons and to Ernest Shackleton's 1907 expedition to the South Pole. James Mackinlay was a co-founder of Glen Mhor Distillery, and bought Glen Albyn at the end of the nineteenth century; both were sold in 1972. The company is now owned by JBB (Greater Europe). As well as The Original, the Mackinlay range also includes 12-year-old and de luxe blends.

Passport

Chivas Brothers,
Paisley

TYPE
Blend

STRENGTH
40%

TASTE RATING
2-3

MINIATURES
Yes

COMMENTS

A well-rounded blend which has the Glen Keith single malt at its core. Sweet, slighty fruity flavours are complemented by a delicate smoky finish.

Chivas Brothers is a subsidiary of the Canadian drinks firm Seagram, by whom it was bought in 1949. The origins of the Chivas Brothers company can be traced back to the establishment of a wine and spirit merchant and licensed grocer in Aberdeen in 1801. Owning nine malt distilleries, Seagram is an important company in the Scotch whisky market. Passport was launched in 1965 after several years' research to produce a blend that would appeal specifically to a younger, less traditional market.

Pinwinnie

Inver House Distillers,
Moffat Distillery, Airdrie,
Lanarkshire

TYPE
De luxe

STRENGTH
40%

TASTE RATING
2–3

MINIATURES
Yes

COMMENTS
A Lowland de luxe blend, Pinwinnie is a very smooth whisky, with sweet, fragrant notes and a nicely rounded finish.

VISITORS
The plant is not open to visitors.

*P*inwinnie's producers, Inver House, also own Knockdhu (producing An Cnoc single malt) and Speyburn-Glenlivet distilleries, and have also recently acquired Pulteney, Balmenach and Balblair Distilleries. Since a management buy-out from its parent company, Publicker Distillers, in 1988, Inver House has been one of the few independent, Scottish-owned companies in the whisky industry. Blending is carried out at their complex at Moffat on the outskirts of Airdrie in the central Lowlands, a converted former paper mill which also holds a grain distillery.

Pittyvaich

Pittyvaich-Glenlivet
Distillery,
Dufftown, Keith, Banffshire

TYPE

Single malt

BOTTLING AGE

12 years

STRENGTH

43%

TASTE RATING

4

MINIATURES

Yes

COMMENTS

Pittyvaich is a Speyside malt with a perfumed fruitiness with a hint of spice and a strong aftertaste.

SPEYSIDE
SINGLE MALT
SCOTCH WHISKY

PITTYVAICH

distillery is situated in the *DULLAN GLEN* on the *outskirts* of Dufftown, near to the *historic Mortlach Church* which dates back to the 6th. The distillery draws water from two nearby

springs - CONVALLEYS and *BALLIEMORE.* Pittyvaich single *MALT SCOTCH WHISKY* has a *perfumed, fruity* nose and a *robust* flavour with a *hint of spiciness.*

AGED **12** YEARS

Distilled & Bottled in SCOTLAND
PITTYVAICH DISTILLERY
Dufftown, Keith, Banffshire, Scotland

43% vol   70 cl

*I*t was the success of neighbouring Dufftown-Glenlivet and the quality of its water supply, from the local Jock's Well, which encouraged Bell to build the brand-new Pittyvaich-Glenlivet Distillery almost next door, in 1974. Almost all of its product now goes into United Distillers' blends, and the single malt was difficult to find until it was officially bottled by UD as part of their Distillery (Flora and Fauna) Malts series. The distillery has now been closed.

Port Ellen

Port Ellen Distillery,
Port Ellen, Islay, Argyll

TYPE
Single malt
BOTTLING AGE
Varies
STRENGTH
Varies
TASTE RATING
3–4
MINIATURES
Yes
COMMENTS

*P*ort Ellen was established in 1824 and stands in the town of the same name in the south of the island. The distillery was closed earlier this century, from 1930 until 1967, when it was re-opened, modernized and enlarged. Its produce has been regarded by some conoisseurs as the classic Islay malt. The distillery, latterly owned by United Distillers, was mothballed in 1984 and has now been closed permanently.

A milder Islay than some, Port Ellen is a basically dry malt with a reasonably mild, smoky and peaty flavour. It is available from independent bottling merchants.

Pride of Islay

Gordon and MacPhail,
Elgin, Moray

TYPE

Vatted malt

BOTTLING AGE

12 years

STRENGTH

40%

TASTE RATING

4

MINIATURES

Yes

COMMENTS

One of Gordon and MacPhail's series of malts capturing the classic characteristics of the leading regions, this is a vatting of the finest whiskies produced on Islay. It has a complex nose with salty, medicinal and smoky flavours, but is mellower than some Islay whiskies.

VISITORS

Gordon and MacPhail's shop South St, Elgin is open 0900–1715 Mon.–Wed. (0900–1300 Wed. in winter), 0830–1715

*G*ordon and MacPhail started in business in 1895 as a licensed grocers and wine and spirit merchant, as had done so many of the foremost names among the Scotch whisky blending industry. Unlike the others, however, Gordon and MacPhail have retained all the original aspects of their business as well as extending into vatting, blending and bottling, and they are today the world's leading malt whisky specialists.

Pride of the Lowlands

Gordon and MacPhail,
Elgin, Moray

TYPE	
Vatted malt	
BOTTLING AGE	
12 years	
STRENGTH	
40%	
TASTE RATING	
2	
MINIATURES	
Yes	

COMMENTS

One of Gordon and MacPhail's series of malts capturing the classic characteristics of the leading regions, this is a vatting of the finest whiskies distilled in the Lowlands, and has a sweet, butterscotch-like nose with a smoky–woody finish.

VISITORS

Gordon and MacPhail's shop South St, Elgin is open 0900–1715 Mon.–Wed. (0900–1300 Wed. in winter), 0830–1715 Thu.–Fri., 0900–1700 Sat.

*G*ordon and MacPhail's premises are located in Elgin on the banks of the River Lossie and close to Speyside, arguably the heart of the Scotch whisky industry. The firm has been in business for almost a century, initially as a licensed grocers and wine and spirit merchants. Their business encompasses the vatting, blending and bottling of whiskies, while their retail shop is among the leading malt whisky shops in the UK.

Pride of Orkney

Gordon and MacPhail,
Elgin, Moray

TYPE

Vatted malt

BOTTLING AGE

12 years

STRENGTH

40%

TASTE RATING

3

MINIATURES

Yes

COMMENTS

One of Gordon and MacPhail's series of malts capturing the classic characteristics of the leading regions, this is a vatting of the finest whiskies produced in Orkney, and is a well-balanced whisky with a sweet, toasted nose, with a hint of heather.

Gordon and MacPhail's premises are located in Elgin on the banks of the River Lossie and close to Speyside, arguably the heart of the Scotch whisky industry. The firm has been in business for almost a century, initially as a licensed grocers and wine and spirit merchants. Their business encompasses the vatting, blending and bottling of whiskies, while their retail shop is among the leading malt whisky shops in the UK.

VISITORS

Gordon and MacPhail's shop South St, Elgin is open 0900–1715 Mon.–Wed. (0900–1300 Wed. in winter), 0830–1715 Thu.–Fri., 0900–1700 Sat.

Pride of Strathspey

Gordon and MacPhail, Elgin, Moray

TYPE	
Vatted malt	
BOTTLING AGE	
12, 25 years	
STRENGTH	
40%	
TASTE RATING	
2	
MINIATURES	
Yes	

COMMENTS

One of Gordon and MacPhail's series of malts capturing the classic characteristics of the leading regions, this is a vatting of the finest whiskies distilled in Strathspey. This malt is a citrus-fruity whisky in nose and palate, with a very pleasant aftertaste.

Gordon and MacPhail started in business in 1895 as a licensed grocers and wine and spirit merchant, as had done so many of the foremost names among the Scotch whisky blending industry. Unlike the others, however, Gordon and MacPhail have retained all the original aspects of their business as well as extending into vatting, blending and bottling, and they are today the world's leading malt whisky specialists.

VISITORS

Gordon and MacPhail's shop South St, Elgin is open 0900–1715 Mon.–Wed. (0900–1300 Wed. in winter), 0830–1715 Thu.–Fri., 0900–1700 Sat.

Rosebank

*Rosebank Distillery,
Camelon, Falkirk,
Stirlingshire*

TYPE

Single malt

BOTTLING AGE

12 years

STRENGTH

43%

TASTE RATING

2

MINIATURES

Yes

COMMENTS

One of the best known Lowland malts, Rosebank is a smooth, mild whisky of light and subtle character, which makes it ideal as a pre-dinner dram.

LOWLAND
SINGLE MALT
SCOTCH WHISKY

*Established on its present
site at CAMELON in 1840*

ROSEBANK

distillery stands on the banks of the *FORTH* and *CLYDE CANAL*. This was once a busy thoroughfare with boats and steamers continually passing by; it is still the source of water for cooling. This single *MALT SCOTCH WHISKY* is *triple distilled* which accounts for its *light distinctive nose* and *well balanced* flavour.

AGED **12** YEARS

Distilled & Bottled in SCOTLAND
ROSEBANK DISTILLERY
Falkirk, Stirlingshire, Scotland

43% vol 70cl

*A*lthough a distillery was operating on this site in 1817, the most recent distillery generally dated from 1840, when much rebuilding took place. It stands on the banks of the Forth and Clyde Canal, on the outskirts of Falkirk. Triple distillation processes were used at Rosebank, which had one wash still and two spirit stills. The distillery is now closed. Its single malt was difficult to obtain, although it has been officially bottled in United Distillers and Vintners' Distillery (Flora and Fauna) Malts series.

HIGHLAND
SINGLE MALT SCOTCH WHISKY

ROYAL BRACKLA

distillery, established in 1812, *&c* lies on the
southern shore of the MORAY FIRTH at *Cawdor* near *Nairn*.
Woods around the *distillery* are home to the *SISKIN*:
although a *shy bird*, it can often be seen *feeding* on conifer *seeds*.

In 1835 a *Royal Warrant* was granted to the *distillery* by King William IV,
who enjoyed the *fresh, grassy, fruity* aroma of this *single malt whisky*.

AGED **10** YEARS

43% vol   70cl

Distilled & Bottled in SCOTLAND. ROYAL BRACKLA DISTILLERY, Cawdor, Nairn, Scotland.

Royal Brackla

*Royal Brackla Distillery,
Cawdor, Nairnshire*

TYPE
Single malt

BOTTLING AGE
10 years

STRENGTH
43%

TASTE RATING
4

MINIATURES
Yes

COMMENTS
A light, fresh, grassy malt with a hint of fruitiness. This single malt can be difficult to find.

VISITORS
Visitors are welcome by appointment. Telephone 016677-404280.

While William IV was known to have enjoyed Brackla's whisky, the distillery has been allowed officially to call itself 'Royal' since 1838, when his neice, the new queen Victoria granted it a Royal Warrant. Founded in 1812, the distillery has been rebuilt and extended several times in the past two centuries, although it is currently mothballed. It is licensed to Bissets, now owned by John Dewar & Sons, and almost all of its produce goes into their blends.

Royal Culross

Gibson Scotch Whisky Distilleries Ltd, Glasgow

TYPE

Vatted malt

BOTTLING AGE

8 years

STRENGTH

43%

TASTE RATING

3–4

MINIATURES

Yes

COMMENTS

Royal Culross is a vatted malt of substantial character and body with a pungent aroma and smooth, malty tones balanced by a lighter, slightly peaty edge.

*R*oyal Culross is one of a range of whiskies, including the popular blend Fraser McDonald and the Scotia Royale deluxe blend, which are associated with the Glen Scotia Distillery in Campbeltown. All three are produced by Gibson Scotch Whisky Distilleries Ltd, a subsidiary of the Loch Lomond Distillery Co. Ltd of Alexandria. The company now has three malt distilleries (Loch Lomond which produces Inchmurrin, a Highland malt, Littlemill, a Lowland malt, and Glen Scotia from Campbeltown) as well as one grain distillery on the site at Alexandria.

Royal Lochnagar

Royal Lochnagar Distillery,
Crathie, Ballater,
Aberdeenshire

TYPE

Single malt

BOTTLING AGE

12 years, no age given
for Selected Reserve

STRENGTH

40%, 43% (Selected Reserve)

TASTE RATING

3–4

MINIATURES

Yes

COMMENTS

A big-bodied, rich and fruity malt with a delightful sherried flavour. Royal Lochnagar Selected Reserve, with a more robust taste, is also available.

VISITORS

Visitors are welcome 1000–1700 Mon.–Sat. and 1200–1600 Easter–Oct.; 1000–1700 Mon.–Fri., Nov.–Easter. Telephone 013397-42273.

Lochnagar Distillery was built in 1826 by James Robertson, an infamous local illicit distiller, on the slopes of the mountain from which it took its name. Distilling was not peaceful work at that time: Lochnagar was destroyed by fire, reputedly the work of rival illicit distillers, in 1841 before being taken over and rebuilt by John Begg four years later Its 'Royal' prefix came after a visit and tasting in 1848 by Queen Victoria (who was said to be partial to whisky) and Prince Albert, who were staying at nearby Balmoral. The distillery was bought by Dewar, is now owned by United Distillers and Vintners and is licensed to John Begg Ltd.

St Magdalene

*St Magdalene Distillery,
Linlithgow, West Lothian*

TYPE

Single malt

BOTTLING AGE

Varies

STRENGTH

Varies

TASTE RATING

2–3

MINIATURES

Yes

COMMENTS

A light-bodied Lowland malt, smooth and generally dry yet with a hint of fruity sweetness. Available only from independent merchants and their retail outlets, its produce can be difficult to find.

*S*t Magdalene, built on the lands of St Mary's Cross towards the end of the nineteenth century, was until recently the sole survivor of the six distilleries which existed in Linlithgow in the last century. Linlithgow had once been a centre of brewing and distilling due to an abundance of barley and fine water from local supplies. All the distillery's production officially went into blends, although it is still available through independent bottlers. St Magdalene was closed by its owners, United Distillers, in the mid 1980s, the building subsequently being converted to private housing.

Scapa

Scapa Distillery,
Kirkwall, Orkney

TYPE	
Single malt	
BOTTLING AGE	
12 years	
STRENGTH	
40%	
TASTE RATING	
3	
MINIATURES	
Yes	

COMMENTS

Scapa is a spicy medium-bodied malt with a heathery flavour which is complemented by a satisfyingly oaky sweetness.

VISITORS

The distillery has no reception centre, but visitors are welcome by appointment. Telephone 01856-872071 to arrange.

Scapa is one of two distilleries in Kirkwall (Highland Park being the other), yet despite their proximity, their whiskies taste quite different. Scapa was built in 1885 by Macfarlane and Townsend – the latter already a well-known distiller on Speyside – and was bought by Hiram Walker in 1954. It is now owned by Allied Distillers who send most of its produce for blending, but also market the single largely through export outlets. The distillery overlooks the giant natural bay of Scapa Flow, a major Royal Navy anchorage in both world wars. The distillery was saved from destruction by fire by ships in the bay during the First World War.

Scotia Royale

*Gibson Scotch Whisky
Distilleries Ltd,
Glasgow*

TYPE
De luxe

BOTTLING AGE
12 years

STRENGTH
40%, 43%

TASTE RATING
2–3

MINIATURES
Yes

COMMENTS
A medium-bodied de luxe blend, Scotia Royale is a smooth, well-balanced whisky with a hint of peat. Glen Scotia malt is one of this whisky's most important ingredients.

Scotia Royale is one of a range of whiskies, including the popular blend Fraser McDonald and Royal Culross vatted malt, which are associated with the Glen Scotia Distillery in Campbeltown. All three are produced by Gibson Scotch Whisky Distilleries Ltd, a subsidiary of the Loch Lomond Distillery Co. Ltd of Alexandria. The company now has three malt distilleries (Loch Lomond which produces Inchmurrin, a Highland malt, Littlemill, a Lowland malt, and Glen Scotia from Campbeltown) as well as one grain distillery on the site at Alexandria.

The Singleton of Auchroisk

Auchroisk Distillery,
Mulben, Banffshire

TYPE
Single malt

BOTTLING AGE
Minimum 10 years

STRENGTH
40%

TASTE RATING
2–3

MINIATURES
Yes

COMMENTS
This whisky is medium-bodied, with a hint of peat to its flavour, which is smooth and sweet, derived from part-maturation in sherry casks.

VISITORS
Visitors are welcome by appointment on weekdays. Telephone 01542-8606333 to arrange.

O ne of the newest Scots whisky distilleries (opened in 1974), Auchroisk was built by International Distillers and Vintners and is licensed to Justerini & Brooks. Dorie's Well provides the distillery with its pure, natural water source. The building itself has won several awards, including one from the Angling Foundation for not interfering with the progress of local salmon as they swim upriver. The company only has been marketing its single malt since 1987 but it is already a winner of twelve major awards.

Speyburn

*Speyburn-Glenlivet
Distillery,
Rothes, Moray*

TYPE
Single malt

BOTTLING AGE
10 years

STRENGTH
40%

TASTE RATING
3–4

MINIATURES
Yes

COMMENTS
A medium-bodied whisky with a firm yet subtle flavour and a dry, warming, peaty finish.

VISITORS
The distillery is not open to visitors.

Speyburn was built in 1897 on the outskirts of Rothes, and outwardly has hardly been altered in the past century. Set among rolling green slopes, it is one of the most picturesque distilleries in Scotland. It was originally built for the blenders John Hopkins and later acquired by United Distillers. Its produce was difficult to find as a single malt until it was bought from UD in 1992 by the independent Inver House Distillers, also producers of An Cnoc malt and Pinwinnie de luxe blend.

Springbank

*Springbank Distillery,
Campbeltown, Argyll*

TYPE

Single malt

BOTTLING AGE

10 years, 21 years

STRENGTH

46%

TASTE RATING

4

MINIATURES

Yes

COMMENTS

Often described as a classic malt, Springbank is a smooth, mellow whisky, light yet complex and full-flavoured. Special bottlings of older Springbanks are available with a 50-year-old due to be released early in 2001.

VISITORS

The distillery is open to visitors strictly by appointment. Telephone 01586-552085 to arrange.

Springbank was built in 1828 by the Mitchell family, previous owners of an illicit still in the area. The distillery is still owned today by the founders' family, and has never been closed at any time in its history. It is presently the only remaining working distillery in Campbeltown, the only Scots town with its own regional whisky classification to reflect the proliferation of distilleries which could be found here in the past. Along with Glenfiddich, Springbank is unusual in bottling on the premises, and is also the only Scottish distillery to carry out the full malt whisky production process, from floor malting to bottling. Springbank is not coloured with caramel, and is the only malt sold under a distillery label which has not been chill filtered. Longrow single malt is also produced here.

Stag's Breath Liqueur

Meikles of Scotland,
Newtonmore, Inverness-shire

TYPE
Liqueur

STRENGTH
19.8%

TASTE RATING
2

MINIATURES
Yes

COMMENTS
A light and smooth union of fine Speyside whisky with heather comb honey. Equally suited to a role as an aperitif or as a digestif.

VISITORS
Meikles have no visitor facilties at present.

Meikles of Scotland is a small Speyside family firm and has been producing Stag's Breath since 1989. The liqueur takes its name from one of the fictional whiskies lost at sea in Sir Compton Mackenzie's famous re-telling of the wartime sinking of the SS *Politician*, in his book, *Whisky Galore*.

EST 1831

RARE SELECTED

STEWARTS CREAM OF THE BARLEY

BLENDED SCOTCH WHISKY

DISTILLED BLENDED & BOTTLED IN SCOTLAND
STEWART & SON OF DUNDEE LIMITED
DUNDEE SCOTLAND
100% SCOTCH WHISKIES

40% vol   70 cl

Stewarts Cream of the Barley

Allied Distillers, Dumbarton, Dunbartonshire

TYPE

Blend

STRENGTH

40%

TASTE RATING

2

MINIATURES

Yes

COMMENTS

A popular, good-quality blend with a soft and well-balanced, sweetish, malty flavour.

VISITORS

Visitors are welcome by appointment.

Stewart & Son of Dundee was founded in 1831 and was one of the first companies to exploit newer methods of distilling – particularly the new patent still – and the beginnings of the market for blended whiskies. The company grew steadily in size and the brand in popularity. It was bought by Allied-Lyons in 1969 and today operates under Allied Distillers as one of their most popular standard blends for the UK market.

Strathisla

Strathisla Distillery,
Keith, Banffshire

TYPE

Single malt

BOTTLING AGE

12 years

STRENGTH

43%

TASTE RATING

4

MINIATURES

Yes

COMMENTS

A big, robust whisky which is full-flavoured and fruity, with a nutty, sherried sweetness.

VISITORS

Visitors are welcome 0930–1600 Mon.–Fri., Feb.–mid-Mar.; 0930–1600 Mon.–Sat., 1230–1600 Sun., mid-Mar.–Nov.

According to records, production of a 'heather ale' by local clerics had been taking place in this area as early as 1208. The later siting of Milton Distillery (as Strathisla was formerly known) here in the eighteenth century may have been for the same reasons: set in a good barley-producing area, with easy access to a pure local spring which had been a holy well of local Cistercian monks, and said to be guarded by water spirits. The distillery, one of the oldest and most picturesque in the Highlands, passed through several hands until it was bought by Chivas Brothers, a Seagram subsidiary, in 1950.

Talisker

Talisker Distillery, Carbost, Isle of Skye

TYPE

Single malt

BOTTLING AGE

8, 10 years

STRENGTH

45.8%

TASTE RATING

5

MINIATURES

Yes

COMMENTS

Talisker is Skye's only malt and has been described as being mid-way between Islay and Highland malts. It is full-bodied with a rich, peaty flavour and elements of malty, fruity sweetness.

VISITORS

Visitors are welcome 0930–1600 Mon.–Fri., Apr.–Jun.; 0930–1630 Mon.–Sat., Jul.–Sept.; 0930–1630 Mon.–Fri., Oct.; 1400–1630 Mon.–Fri., Nov.–Mar. Telephone 01478-640314.

*T*alisker Distillery had an inauspicious start in the 1830s, being denounced by a local minister as a great curse for the area. Despite his disapproval, distilling has continued successfully, with the distillery changing hands several times. A victim of several fires throughout its 160-year history, it was almost completely rebuilt in 1960. The distillery is owned today by United Distillers and Vintners, and some of its product goes into Johnnie Walker blends. The single malt appears in UDV's Classic Malts series, and was even praised by exile Robert Louis Stevenson in his poem, *The Scotsman's Return from Abroad*, as one of 'The King o' drinks'.

The Talisman

J. & W. Hardie
Glasgow

TYPE

Blend

BOTTLING AGE

5 years

STRENGTH

40%, 43%

MINIATURES

Yes

COMMENTS

The Talisman is an exceptionally smooth blend with hints of apple and a slightly peaty aroma.

*T*he Talisman is produced at the Tomatin Distillery near Inverness, which is not only one of the highest in the country (at around 1000 feet in the Monadhliath mountains) but also has the largest capacity, with production as high as 5 million gallons per annum. The Talisman takes its name from the novel by Sir Walter Scott, as does The Antiquary, its sister blend in the Tomatin portfolio. It is a blend of more than 25 whiskies, drawn from distilleries from throughout Scotland. The youngest of these is 5 years old with the heart of the blend being 8-year-old malts.

Tamdhu

Tamdhu Distillery,
Knockando, Aberlour,
Banffshire

TYPE

Single malt

BOTTLING AGE

No age given

STRENGTH

40%

TASTE RATING

2–3

MINIATURES

Yes

COMMENTS

*H*ighland Distilleries (now Highland Distillers) bought this distillery shortly after it opened in 1897 and have owned it ever since. It was extensively refurbished in the 1970s and is now one of the most modern distilleries on Speyside. Set in the Spey valley, Tamdhu used to favour the hyphenated Glenlivet suffix, but this has been dropped in recent years. As well as its appearance as a single malt, Tamdhu also features in Highland Distillers' The Famous Grouse blend.

A good, light-to-medium Speyside malt, which is slightly peaty but with a delicate sweetness and a long, subtle finish.

VISITORS

The distillery is not open to visitors.

Tamnavulin

Tamnavulin Distillery,
Tomnavoulin, Banffshire

TYPE

Single malt

BOTTLING AGE

12 years

STRENGTH

40%

TASTE RATING

3

MINIATURES

Yes

COMMENTS

A lightish, mellow Glenlivet-type malt with a sweetish bouquet and taste but an underlying grapey note.

Opened in 1966, this was one of the newest Highland distilleries. A rather functional building, it is set on slopes above the River Livet and used water from a nearby burn. This is another distillery which once carried the hyphenated Glenlivet suffix but has since shed it. Tamnavulin was owned until 1993 by Invergordon Distillers, but Whyte & Mackay acquired the group that year. Since then production has been moth-balled here and at two of the other former Invergordon malt distilleries, Tullibardine and Bruichladdich.

Teacher's Highland Cream

Allied Distillers, Dumbarton, Dunbartonshire

TYPE

Blend

STRENGTH

40%, 43%

TASTE RATING

2

MINIATURES

Yes

COMMENTS

Teacher's Highland Cream is a superior blend which has a smooth, sweet flavour with a trace of dryer, heathery notes. It is one of the most popular blended whiskies in the UK. Its sister blend is the 12-year-old Teacher's Royal Highland.

VISITORS

Visitors are welcome by appointment.

The Teacher's company was begun in Glasgow in the 1830s by William Teacher, a young man barely in his twenties. The business started with licensed premises where people could drink whisky, and expanded through the years of the nineteenth century to include blending, bottling and export interests. Highland Cream was first marketed in 1884, although Teacher's did not build its first distillery, at Ardmore, until 1898. The company later concentrated on blending, bottling and exporting, selling off its licensed shops. Today the company is owned by Allied Distillers and the blend sells into 150 countries.

Teaninich

*Teaninich Distillery,
Alness, Ross-shire*

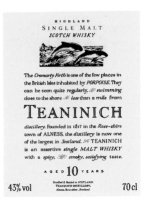

HIGHLAND
SINGLE MALT
SCOTCH WHISKY

The *Cromarty Firth* is one of the few places in the British Isles inhabited by *PORPOISE*. They can be seen quite regularly, swimming close to the shore *less* than a *mile* from

TEANINICH

distillery. Founded in 1817 in the *Ross-shire* town of ALNESS, the *distillery* is now one of the largest in *Scotland.* TEANINICH is an assertive *single* MALT WHISKY with a *spicy,* smoky, *satisfying* taste.

AGED **10** YEARS

Distilled & Bottled in SCOTLAND
TEANINICH DISTILLERY,
Alness, Ross-shire, Scotland

43% vol   70 cl

TYPE

Single malt

BOTTLING AGE

10 years

STRENGTH

43%

TASTE RATING

3

MINIATURES

Yes

COMMENTS

A difficult-to-find single malt, Teaninich is assertive with a spicy, smoky and satisfying taste.

VISITORS

The distillery is not open to visitors.

*T*eaninich Distillery dates from the early 1800s and in 1887 it was recorded as the only distillery north of Inverness to be 'lighted by electricity'. The majority of the present buildings date from the 1970s and it is now owned by United Distillers and Vintners who reopened it in 1990 after it was mothballed for several years. Most of the production has traditionally gone into blending, but the single malt has become easier to find since its official bottling as part of UDV's Distillery (Flora and Fauna) Malts series.

Tobermory

Tobermory Distillery,
Tobermory, Isle of Mull

TYPE	
Single malt	
BOTTLING AGE	
10 years	
STRENGTH	
40%	
TASTE RATING	
3	
MINIATURES	
Yes	

COMMENTS

Set in a wooded site by the sea, Mull's only distillery has enjoyed mixed fortunes since distilling began in 1798. The distillery dates back to 1823 and it has been closed several times during its existence, most recently in the 1980s when it was mothballed. Having reopened in 1990, the distillery is now back in production. The distillery was previously known as Ledaig but changed its name in the 1970s; a single malt marketed under the old name is available. Tobermory remains one of the few family-owned independent distilleries, under the control of Burn Stewart Distillers.

A nicely balanced, light malt with a delicate, flowery aroma and drier, heathery tones in its flavour. A good pre-dinner dram.

VISITORS

The Visitor Centre and Distillery Shop are open Mon.–Fri., Easter–30 Sept. Tours can be arranged at other times in the year. Telephone 01688-302645.

Tomatin

Tomatin Distillery,
Tomatin, Inverness-shire

TYPE

Single malt

BOTTLING AGE

10, 12, 30 years

STRENGTH

40%, 43%

TASTE RATING

2

MINIATURES

Yes

COMMENTS

A lightly-peated and delicately flavoured malt which makes a pleasant aperitif.

VISITORS

Visitors are welcome 0900–1630 Mon.–Fri., all year, and 0900–1300 Sat., May–Oct. Large parties must book in advance. Telephone 01808-511444.

At over 1000 feet above sea level, Tomatin is one of Scotland's highest distilleries. Situated in the Monadhliath Mountains from where it draws its water supply, the distillery was established in 1897 (although it is known that whisky has been made on the site since the sixteenth century). A major programme of expansion in the early 1970s made Tomatin the largest distillery in Scotland. Against a background of general decline in the industry, however, the company experienced financial difficulties in the 1980s before being bought by a Japanese consortium, thus becoming the first Scotch whisky distillery to have Japanese owners.

Tomintoul

Tomintoul Distillery,
Ballindalloch, Banffshire

TYPE

Single malt

BOTTLING AGE

10 years

STRENGTH

40%

TASTE RATING

2–3

MINIATURES

Yes

COMMENTS

A light, delicate whisky with a
fine balance of flavours in the
Glenlivet style. An ideal dram
for beginners, or as an aperitif.

VISITORS

The distillery is not open to
visitors.

*B*uilt in 1964 near to Tomintoul,
the second-highest village in
Scotland and once a centre for illicit
distilling, Tomintoul Distillery is also,
at 1100 feet, one of the highest in the
country. Its water is drawn from the
nearby Ballantruan spring. In spite of
its scenic location, surrounded by hills
and the Glenlivet forest, it is a
modern, functional building which
lacks the charm associated with the
architecture of many older distilleries.
Owned until 1993 by Invergordon
Distillers, Tomintoul was one of the
group's seven malt distilleries which
passed into the hands of Whyte &
Mackay – now JBB (Greater Europe) –
that year.

The Tormore

The Tormore Distillery, Advie, Grantown-on-Spey, Moray

TYPE

Single malt

BOTTLING AGE

10 years

STRENGTH

40%, 43%

TASTE RATING

2–3

MINIATURES

Yes

COMMENTS

A medium-bodied whisky, rich and slightly nutty in flavour. An after-dinner dram.

VISITORS

Visitors are welcome by appointment. Telephone 01807-510244.

*B*uilt in 1959, this was Speyside's first new distillery this century. Not a traditional-looking distillery, it is an attractive complex in a pleasant Highland setting, and has the delightfully kitsch touch of a chiming clock which plays the air *Highland Laddie* every hour. Tormore's water comes from the Achvochkie Burn, fed by the nearby Loch an Oir (Lake of Gold). An impressive working model of the Tormore Distillery can be seen at the Scotch Whisky Heritage Centre on Edinburgh's Royal Mile. The distillery itself is owned by Allied Distillers, with some of its produce featuring in their Long John blends.

216

Tullibardine

Tullibardine Distillery,
Blackford, Perthshire

TYPE	
Single malt	
BOTTLING AGE	
10 years	
STRENGTH	
40%	
TASTE RATING	
2–3	
MINIATURES	
Yes	
COMMENTS	

*T*ullibardine Distillery was built on the site of a medieval brewery reputed to have produced ale for the coronation of James IV in 1488. It was opened as a distillery in 1949 and is actually situated at Blackford, a few miles away from Tullibardine village. Tullibardine was one of the seven malt distilleries, _previously belonging to Invergordon Distillers, which in 1993 passed into the ownership of Whyte & Mackay, now known as JBB (Greater Europe). Since then production has been mothballed.

Tullibardine is a good, all-round single malt, full-bodied and with a sweet, well-rounded flavour with a fruity richness.

Ultima

Justerini & Brooks,
London

TYPE

Blend

STRENGTH

43%

TASTE RATING

3

MINIATURES

No

COMMENTS

Ultima is the ultimate blend
and a truly unique creation: a
blend of 116 malts and 12 grain
whiskies, many of which are no
longer being produced. Ultima
has a rich, slightly sweet aroma
with a smooth, dry finish.

*J*usterini & Brooks' principal
founder, Giacomo Justerini, was a
wine merchant from Bologna who was
infatuated by an Italian opera singer,
whom he followed to London in the
mid-eighteenth century. He set up the
wine merchants, Justerini and Brooks
in the capital in 1749 and began selling
Scotch thirty years later. In 1962 the
company built on previous amalgamations by combining with W. & A.
Gilbey to form International Distillers
and Vintners Ltd (IDV). Grand
Metropolitan bought IDV, then part of
Watney Mann & Truman, in 1972. The
creation of Ultima represented the
fulfilment of a dream held for many
years by J&B's Master Blender, Jim
Milne.

WM.
SANDERSON
& SON. LTD

EDINBURGH
SCOTLAND

BY APPOINTMENT TO HER MAJESTY QUEEN ELIZABETH II
SCOTCH WHISKY DISTILLERS

FINEST SCOTCH WHISKY

VAT 69 ®

Wm Sanderson Son.
DISTILLERS, EDINBURGH, SCOTLAND

43°   750 ml

DISTILLED AND BOTTLED IN SCOTLAND

Vat 69

United Distillers and Vintners,
Kilmarnock, Ayrshire

TYPE
Blend

STRENGTH
43%

TASTE RATING
2

MINIATURES
Yes

COMMENTS

A smooth, well-balanced and distinctly mature blend, light but with a pleasantly malty background.

Sandersons were Leith wine and spirit merchants who moved into whisky blending in the 1860s. William Sanderson was keen to find a notable blend to market and produced 100 different whiskies to be tested, each in numbered casks. The unanimous choice of his associates was the whisky from vat number 69, and so the name suggested itself. It was introduced onto the market in 1882, and William Sanderson's son was responsible for early advertising and marketing successes. Sanderson was also a founder of the North British Distillery company in 1885, ensuring supplies of good grain whisky for his blends. Today Sanderson and its brands are owned by United Distillers and Vintners.

Wallace

Burn Stewart Distillers, Glasgow

TYPE

Liqueur

STRENGTH

35%

TASTE RATING

2

MINIATURES

Yes

COMMENTS

A combination of Deanston's single malt, fruit and herbs, this rich liqueur has a delicate texture with a hint of honey.

*T*his new liqueur is named after the hero of the phenomenally successful film, *Braveheart*. Sir William Wallace, the Guardian of Scotland, secured a famous victory over the English in 1297 at the Battle of Stirling Bridge. The battle site is very close to Deanston Distillery whose malt is a major component of the liqueur. Originally a cotton mill dating back to 1785, Deanston was converted to a distillery in 1966 and draws water from the nearby River Teith. It was bought by Burn Sewart Distillers in 1991.

White Horse

United Distillers and Vintners,
Glasgow

TYPE
Blend

STRENGTH
43%

TASTE RATING
2–3

MINIATURES
Yes

COMMENTS
White Horse is a smooth and distinctive whisky with peaty elements in both its aroma and flavour. It is the leading standard blend in Japan.

White Horse Distillers, known until 1924 as Mackie & Co., was established by James Logan Mackie in 1861. The company became successful under its second head, Peter Mackie, entrepreneur and the driving force who registered the name 'White Horse', called after a famous Edinburgh coaching inn, for his blend in 1890. By the time he died in 1924 his whisky was one of the foremost blends in the world. Three years later White Horse Distillers joined the Distillers Company Ltd, with whom Mackie had had difficult relations during his lifetime. White Horse also produce Logan and White Horse Extra Fine, de luxe blends for the export market.

Whyte & Mackay

JBB (Greater Europe) plc, Glasgow

TYPE

Blend

STRENGTH

43%

TASTE RATING

2

MINIATURES

Yes

COMMENTS

A good quality, smooth, light-bodied whisky with a well-rounded, mellow sweetness. This is said to come from the particular blending process the company uses, vatting the component malts together in sherry butts for at least six months, and then adding the grain content before leaving the resulting blend to mature further.

James Whyte and Charles Mackay, both whisky merchants, began their partnership and blending firm in 1844. Sales and the company expanded steadily throughout the late nineteenth century and into the twentieth, although their main markets were always overseas. Made to the same recipe since 1844, Whyte and Mackay contains over forty of thehighest malt and grain whiskies and is matured twice to produce its distinctive smooth taste. Although it is available in over 100 countries, the UK remains its strongest market and the whisky was given a distinctive new blue branding in 1998

Irish

The History of Whiskey-making in Ireland

*T*he origins of whiskey making in Ireland are just as obscure as in its Scots cousin. The traditional folktales too, which have grown up to guesstimate at its origins are not dissimilar: visitors to Arab lands – this time, sixth-century missionary monks – are credited with having the good sense to return with the secrets of their hosts' distillation processes.

As with the Scots Gaelic, the Irish Gelic term *uisce beatha* is the root of the drink's anglicized name. The story goes that the first to begin the process of anglicization were Ireland's English invaders, the forces of Henry II who first arrived in 1170 AD.

To borrow an Italian saying, if the stories are not true, they are a happy invention, and the real tale will undoubtedly never be known. In any case, by the sixteenth century whiskey production and consumption was widespread. It would not be fanciful to suggest that every area had its own still and the drink was a commonplace of Irish life, whether for its medicinal properties or for simply for the pleasure of drinking it. Consumption spread beyond Ireland, too: Elizabeth I of England was known to be fond of whiskey and one of her more famous courtiers, Sir Walter Raleigh, was the glad recipient of a cask as he set off on his travels. It was well enough travelled even to reach the court of the Russian tsar, Peter the Great.

Taxes on Irish whiskey were introduced in the mid-seventeenth century after the English Civil War by a cash-strapped government in London, and while their enforcement was ineffective enough to be subverted by bribery, stealth or simply by ignoring them, the new laws and duties did serve to disrupt the unofficial industry, with transgressors facing the threat of severe fines and imprisonment. This is not to suggest that all whiskey producers in Ireland instantly chose to go illegal to escape the exciseman: Ireland claims the distinction of having the world's oldest licensed whiskey distillery. At Bushmills in Co. Antrim there had been a tradition of distilling for centuries, and the first licence was granted in 1608. But generally, as over the water in Scotland, the smaller, illicit stills outnumbered their legal counterparts

The world's oldest licenced distillery, 'Old Bushmills' (Irish Distillers)

and the industry continued to grow until, by the end of the eighteenth century, it was thought that there were up to 2000 stills in the country.

As with the Scotch industry, the Excise Act of 1823 proved a turning point. It overhauled and simplified the tax system, encouraged bigger producers to take out licences, and outlawed stills under 40-gallons' capacity, those being the most likely to be illegal. Some of the bigger producers, most notably the Dublin family concerns such as Jameson and Power, grabbed the opportunity to capitalise on their already high reputations, increase the size of their operations and consolidate their share of the spirits market. By the late nineteenth century the future of Irish whiskey looked bright: it was among the most popular spirits in the western world, and by the time the Phylloxera blight struck French vineyards in the 1806s, decimating supplies of brandy, there were over 150 Irish distillers producing over 400 brands, who were able to seize an advantage from the situation. But developments were already taking place which would ultimately see Scotch whisky, considered by the Irish to be an inferior product, outstrip it in the marketplace.

The Irish distillers were to prove themselves singularly unable to read new developments in their market in the coming decades. The first significant event was the invention by Aeneas Coffey, the former Irish Inspector General of Excise, of a continuous patent still. Patented in 1832, the Coffey, or patent still produced a light grain spirit which could be used in a mix with malt whiskey to mellow its full-bodied flavour for the untutored palate. The Irish producers' disdain for such a new departure was not shared by the makers of Scotch, who seized the chance to adulterate their fierier spirit into a more widely acceptable blended product. Although generally acknowledged as having a finer flavour, Irish whiskey, with producers content to rest on their laurels, began to be caught and overtaken in the popularity stakes by the new, aggressively marketed Scotch blends.

An unexpected blow came from the political situation in Ireland. Residual bad feeling after the War of Independence and a bruising trade war between Britain and the new Irish Free State denied the whiskey industry access to Britain and its imperial markets from the early 1920s.

An already bad state of affairs was worsened by developments in the United States, one of the biggest markets for Irish. The Prohibition laws on the sale of alcohol, in force from 1920 to 1933, hit the Irish industry hard and, ironically, whiskey's very popularity ultimately served to give it a bad name in the US. When supplies of the legal stuff ran out, American bootleggers didn't hesitate to call their illicitly distilled fire-water by Irish names to capitalise on the real spirit's popularity. Inevitably its reputation suffered, but the real body-blow in the American market was dealt yet again by the Irish producers' inability to anticipate developments: maturing stocks had been allowed to run down during the Prohibition period, with the result that the industry was unable to meet the return to full demand in 1933. The Scotch blended industry suffered fewer such problems, and it swallowed up the market share of Irish in the US.

These errors of judgement and historical accident together

depressed the fortunes of Irish whiskey for several decades. Although the spirit continued to be as popular as ever at home, export markets virtually dried up and the industry atrophied, with some smaller and medium-sized distilleries closing for good. A turnaround finally began in 1966 when the South's largest distilleries joined forces to create the Irish Distillers Group. The addition a few years later of Bushmills from the North ensured a concentration of all-Irish marketing power. One instantly recognisable result of the amalgamation was that all Irish whiskey was henceforth spelled with 'ey' rather than simply 'y'. Previously a practice followed only by the Dublin producers, it now gave Irish an extra, visual distinction from Scotch.

The unfortunate attempts by rival groups at take overs in the Scotch industry were mirrored in the late 1980s in Ireland, with the French Pernod Ricard group ultimately emerging victorious in their attempts to buy Irish Distillers. Irish Distillers' successes, particularly with Bushmills and Jamesons, have been built on by the new owners, raising the profile of Irish whiskey once more beyond its native shores. Whiskey and whiskey lovers everywhere will look for these trends to continue.

The Making of Irish Whiskey

*T*he basic processes and ingredients used in the making of Irish and Scotch whiskies are not dissimilar. Both, of course, observe the traditional steps: malting, mashing, fermentation, distillation and maturation, but it is from the small differences in approach at crucial points that the variations in the taste and character of two spirits lie.

Pot Still Whiskey

(1) **Malting** At the outset, the Irish process varies noticeably from the Scotch. Although barley is the main ingredient of both, the Irish treatment is quite different. The sprouted

Barley being sent to the Jameson Bow St. Distillery, c. 1920 (Irish Distillers)

barley in Irish whiskey is dried in the closed kiln, not over a peat fire – perhaps surprisingly, as Ireland has such an abundance of the fuel. This is then mixed with unmalted barley before being ground into grist. A nineteenth-century tax on malt first encouraged the use of unmalted barley, a necessity-driven innovation which happily proved its worth over the years. The absence of peat-smokiness mixed with the unmalted barley already promise a spirit with a distinct flavour and character.

(2) **Mashing** The processes involved in grinding the grain into grist and then mixing it with water in the mash tun to produce wort are the same in both Irish and Scotch production.

(3) **Fermentation** Once again, the same basic steps are followed in the two procedures: with the wort in the washback, yeast is added to convert the liquid's sugars into alcohol.

(4) **Distillation** The essential principles and processes of distillation are unchanging, whatever the drink being produced, or level of skill of the distiller, or still

Copper pot stills used in the triple distillation of Irish whiskey (Irish Distillers)

being used. The alcohol, with its lower boiling point than water, is steamed off. As with Scotch, the shape of the still also has a part to play in the whiskey's final character, and the Irish stills are generally larger than the Scottish ones. This distilling would generally happen twice in Scotland. But at this stage also, Irish whiskey is usually (although not always) given the further refinement of a third pass through the still. With even more of the lower alcohols left behind, a subtly different-tasting, purer and lighter alcohol is emerging.

(5) **Maturation** The final stage in the production process is the same as for any spirit: the whiskey is transferred into casks to mature for the required number of years – three at legal minimum but more likely to be eight, ten or even longer for some of the top brands. The casks have usually had other occupants – normally sherry, bourbon or rum – although new

Whiskey ageing in oak barrels in the Old Bushmills warehouse (Irish Distillers)

oak casks are also used. Each wood imparts its own flavour, and the final resulting blend in a bottle can be a mix of hundreds of casks.

Grain Whiskey

The processes followed in Ireland for the manufacture of grain whiskey are basically the same as in Scotland. Again, different cereals can be used – wheat, maize and a large proportion of unmalted barley, with distillation taking place in two patent stills. The resulting grain spirit is predominately used in Irish blends. At Midleton Distillery in Co. Cork, the patent stills are also used in conjunction with the pot stills, with the result that some of their whiskey has been distilled five times.

Blending

Although the whiskies in Scotch blends can be 'married' in casks for a year or more to allow infusion of the flavours, in Ireland they are vatted together for a matter of days at most. According to the accepted wisdom in Ireland, this reflects the relative importance of blending in Scotch whisky, where the skills of the blender are crucial to the final product. In Ireland, the theory goes, it is the distiller's art rather than that of the blender's which has by far the greater influence on the whiskey's final taste.

Their disdain for blended, or vatted, whiskies was one of the reasons why Irish distillers lost out in the battle with Scotch for the hearts and favours of the world's whiskey-drinkers. The Irish refused even to recognise the adulterated Scots product as proper whiskey until after it was decreed legitimate by a Royal Commission reporting in 1909. Even until relatively recently, Irish whiskey was sold as pot-still whiskey with no other variation. Now, however, the market is dominated by quality blended whiskies, in response to modern preferences for lighter spirits, and the practice of using mixers with drinks.

Visiting Irish Distilleries

*A*lthough Ireland has a limited number of whiskey-industry centres, most cater well for visitors and tourists. The Irish Whiskey Tourist Trail takes in the two ICD distilleries, north and south, as well as offering a glimpse into the whiskey industry's glorious past.

At Bushmills in Co. Antrim, close to the Giant's Causeway, is Old Bushmills Distillery, offering a guided tour of the distillery and a chance to sample and buy its produce. The distillery is open to visitors from April–October 0900–1730 from Monday–Saturday, and 1200–1730 on Sundays ; out of season, from November–March five tours daily (Monday–Friday) at 1030, 1130, 1330, 1430,and 1530. Telephone 01265-731521 for details. There is an entry fee.

In Dublin is The Old Jameson Distillery at Bow Street where you will find audio-visual presentations, a guided tour of the old distillery and of course, a bar with tasting session and an opportunity to buy some of your favourites. It is open 0930–1800 seven days a week, all year round. Group tours can be booked in advance; telephone 01 88072355. There is an entry fee.

Finally, in Midleton, Co. Cork, is The Old Midleton Distillery, with plenty of fittings still *in situ* in the well-explained walk-around site. A bar and shop round off the facilities. The centre is open 0930–1730 Monday–Sunday, from

March–October, and 1200–1500 Mon.–Sun., from November–February. Telephone to check definite opening dates at the beginning and end of the season; telephone 021 613594. There is an entry fee and special rates for groups.

Not on the ICD trail, but well worth a visit for anyone interested in the whiskey industry, social history or industrial archaeology, is Locke's Distillery Museum at Kilbeggan, Co. Westmeath. The distillery was established in 1757, and its machinery dates from Victorian times. It has been restored and opened by the local community – a task which is ongoing – and is a too-unsung highlight of any trip to the Midlands. The centre is open 0900–1800 daily, May–October, 1000–1600 daily from November–March. Groups are asked to telephone in advance; telephone: 0506-32134.

Poteen

*A*n illicit spirit almost as well-known as its legal equivalent, poteen is so famous that there can hardly be a drinker who has not heard of it. Poteen (or, in Irish, *poitín*, pronounced 'pocheen', with the 'o' sound as in 'pot') has been produced for as long as Irish whiskey has been subject to taxes and laws, and its fame and democratic, accessible nature have secured its place in Irish popular culture. Poteen itself cannot be called whiskey, not least because a much wider variety of ingredients than simply barley can be used (and generally are) and, of course, it is never left for the three years deemed necessary in law to produce a properly matured whiskey!

An illicit poteen still, as depicted in the 1840s

Illicit distillation in most countries was in the past the subject of bitter battles between the distillers and the authorities, and Irish poteen production was no different. An often desperate economic situation for ordinary Irish countrydwellers combined with a British government always vigorous in its dealings with Irish transgressions, to produce several bloody encounters. In the middle were the excisemen: those unlucky enough to be caught by desperate locals might be fortunate to escape with their lives. Anaeas Coffey was seized by such a band and, but for the timely intervention of some troops, would not have lived long enough to invent his patent still.

Generally a colourless liquid, poteen is fiery-tasting and, by nature, less thoroughly distilled than commercially produced whiskies. This lack of precise distillation techniques can be a danger in itself: Brendan Behan related the story of how, during one of his spells in prison, he and his fellow inmates had made their own 'potheen', and a debate had arisen as to the merits of giving the first three drops to the fairies. The more superstitious among them had won out which, as he later discovred, was just as well: 'the first three drops contain a lot of fusel oil which is likely to blind you if you drink it'. Unfortunately even today drinkers are known to have been killed by drinking the foreshots, or by an over-indulgence in poteen itself.

If this has only whetted your appetite to try poteen for yourself but you lack a first-hand supply, commercial versions have been produced. But surely best, and much more interesting and fun, is to find a real-life producer, sit back, and enjoy. You will, after all, be experiencing a piece of authentic Irish.

The Whiskies of Ireland

Taste Rating

The discussions on the different whiskies which follow contain a taste rating of 1–5. This is not intended to be a judgement on the quality or relative standard of the spirit, nor is it possible to place strength and flavour together satisfactorily. Rather, it can be used as an indicator of accessibility of the whisky for a relatively inexperienced palate. A whisky may be mild or strong and still either lack flavour or exude it, so this rating concerns the degree of flavour, while at the same time allowing for the strength interfering with a person's ability to appreciate the flavour. The basic categories are as follows:

1   Popular with particular palates; spirituous, with a very mild flavour

2   Good for beginners; appealing taste and flavour for most palates at certain times

2–3 Also good for beginners, but a little stronger than **2**. One to return to again and again

3   A dram for everyone; not too powerful, with pleasant sensations

3–4 This should also appeal to most tastes, but is slightly stronger, so the palate requires a little more experience

4   Very pleasing; a stronger spirit, ideal for those with more experience

5   Robust; only for the well developed palate

Baileys

R. & A. Bailey & Co., Dublin

TYPE

Cream liqueur

STRENGTH

17%

TASTE RATING

2

MINIATURES

Yes

COMMENTS

Baileys' raisiny-sweet chocolate richness is given added depth by its lingering, whiskey finish.

VISITORS

The plant is not open to visitors.

First of the Irish cream liqueurs on the market, Baileys has never surrendered its position as pack leader. Launched in 1974, it has been for several years the world's leading liqueur brand and is a product so phenomenally successful that it currently accounts for 1% of Ireland's total export trade. The company is a Gilbey's subsidiary, its name chosen as classically Irish, its product an ingenious coupling of two famous Irish products, cream and whiskey. The whiskey is supplied by Irish Distillers, the cream comes from Co. Cavan and both are blended and bottled in Dublin. The company also produces a lower-calorie and lower-fat Baileys Light, aimed mainly at the US market.

Black Bush

Old Bushmills Distillery,
Bushmills, Co. Antrim

TYPE
Blend

STRENGTH
40%

TASTE RATING
2–3

MINIATURES
Yes

COMMENTS
Bushmills' premier blend,Black Bush is a smooth, complex whiskey whose malty nose and mellow, nutty flavours are rounded off with a mellow, sherry-sweet finish.. It secured the Gold Medal at the 1997 International WIne & Spirit Competition in London

VISITORS
Visitors are welcome 0900–1730 Mon.–Sat., 1200–1730 Sun. Apr.–Oct.; Nov.–Mar. Mon.–Fri. five tours daily at 1030, 1130, 1330, 1430, 1530. Telephone 01265-731521.

*O*f the many 'characters' to have had a hand in Irish distilling, Samuel Boyd, owner of Old Bushmills Distillery in the 1920s, is among the most intriguing. He fitted perfectly the stereotype of the aloof, self-made Scotch-Irishman. His pro-temperance sympathies – he was even thought to write campagning leaflets in his spare time, and never allowed drink in his house – sat oddly alongside a career in the spirits trade in which he rose by his efforts to owning his own wholesale company as well as Bushmills. The distillery benefitted from his middle-class, strict, Victorian approach: although working conditions were never luxurious, his unflamboyant, steady-as-she-goes style was able to set the company on a sound footing, in the process beginning a family connection lasting three generations.

Established 1842

CADENHEAD'S

AUTHENTIC COLLECTION

150th anniversary commemoration

Irish Whiskey

This whiskey has been bottled from a selected individual cask
in its natural state and shows the character of that cask.
It has not been diluted with water. It has not been reacted to
change its colour and is free from all additives. It has
not been subjected to any filtration that might remove
natural constituents and spoil its flavour.
It is the authentic product of its Distillery.

Bottled by Wm. Cadenhead, 32 Union Street, Campbeltown,
SCOTLAND

From
JAMIESON'S   No.

BOW STREET DISTILLERY

Distilled in 1963 and bottled in 1991
Matured in an oak cask

750ml   for **27** years   68.1%alc/vol

Bow Street

*Bow Street Distillery,
Dublin*

TYPE
Single-distillery Irish whiskey

BOTTLING AGE
Varies

STRENGTH
Varies

TASTE RATING
3

MINIATURES
Yes

COMMENTS
A smooth, sweet Irish whiskey with fragrant and fruity notes. An ideal after-dinner drink.

VISITORS
Visitors are welcome to The Old Jameson Distillery, Bow St, 0930–1730 Mon.–Sun., all year. Telephone 01 8072355.

$\mathcal{E}$stablished as a distillery before John Jameson bought it over around 1780, Bow Street had originally been owned by the Steins, another famous family of distillers. But it was under its new owners that the distillery became renowned. As sales of whiskey grew throughout the nineteenth century, the industry's good health was mirrored in the buoyancy of Jameson & Son. At one time the company had over a million gallons of whiskey maturing in Bow Street's cellars which wove rabbit-warren-like under the streets north of the Liffey. But by the mid-twentieth century the old site was too cramped, and the decision was taken after Jameson's merger with the Irish Distillers Group to move distilling to Midleton.

Bushmills

Old Bushmills Distillery,
Bushmills, Co. Antrim

TYPE
Blend

STRENGTH
40%

TASTE RATING
2

MINIATURES
Yes

COMMENTS
A fresh-bodied whiskey with a light, pleasant flavour and a hint of malty sweetness in the finish. This is the standard blend of the distillery.

VISITORS
Visitors are welcome 0900–1730 Mon.–Sat., 1200–1730 Sun. Apr.–Oct.; Nov.–Mar. Mon.–Fri. five tours daily at 1030, 1130, 1330, 1430, 1530. Telephone 01265-731521.

Old Bushmills glories in the status of the oldest licensed distillery in the world. It is thought that distilling may have begun on the site as early as the thirteenth century, but the first permit was granted by James VI and I to Sir Thomas Phillipps, a local landowner, in 1608. The site was especially well suited for its purpose, standing on the banks of St Columb's Rill, or stream, which flowed over the nearby peaty ground and into the River Bush, and which still provides the distillery with its fresh water supplies today. Belying its antiquity, Old Bushmills is distinctly Victorian-Speyside in appearance – a legacy of its rebuilding and the addition of its pagoda towers after a devastating fire in 1885.

Bushmills
Distillery Reserve

Old Bushmills Distillery,
Bushmills, Co. Antrim

TYPE
De luxe blend

BOTTLING AGE
12 years

STRENGTH
43%

TASTE RATING
2–3

MINIATURES
No

COMMENTS

Available only from the distillery, this is a very smooth and honey-rich whiskey with spicy and fruity undertones, a pleasant sweet nutty taste and a strong, dry finish.

VISITORS

Visitors are welcome 0900–1730 Mon.–Sat., 1200–1730 Sun. Apr.–Oct.; Nov.–Mar. Mon.–Fri. five tours daily at 1030, 1130, 1330, 1430, 1530. Telephone 01265-731521.

Now owned by the Pernod Ricard group, Old Bushmills Distillery has been through several turns of fortune and sets of owners since its founding as a company in 1783. Its initially mixed fortunes were the result of strong local competition from several distillers, many of them illegal! The distillery was closed and re-opened several times and by the turn of the century the company was no stranger to the receivers despite its by-then award-winning whiskies. Its fortunes revived under the ownership of the Boyd family, but after the Second World War it moved inevitably from being a family concern through a succession of larger, corporate buyers until in 1972 it finally joined with the Irish Distillers Group. IDG themselves were bought by Pernod Ricard at the end of the 1980s.

Bushmills 10 Years Old Malt

Old Bushmills Distillery, Bushmills, Co. Antrim

TYPE
Single malt

BOTTLING AGE
10 years

STRENGTH
40%

TASTE RATING
2–3

MINIATURES
Yes

COMMENTS
Winner of a Gold Medal at the 1997 World Spirits Championships, Bushmills Malt has a rich, sweet and malty flavour and a pleasingly dry finish.

VISITORS
Visitors are welcome 0900–1730 Mon.–Sat., 1200–1730 Sun. Apr.–Oct.; Nov.–Mar. Mon.–Fri. five tours daily at 1030, 1130, 1330, 1430, 1530. Telephone 01265-731521.

Old Bushmills Distillery has enjoyed some sound management and a share of luck throughout its history. But at the backbone of its survival and successes has been the quality of the spirit it has produced, with a portfolio of distinguished whiskies across the production spectrum. In 1897 the distillery marked Queen Victoria's diamond jubilee by its first production of pure malt, specially produced whiskey which retailed at fifty shillings a case! (For many years in the past century Bushmills proudly proclaimed its status as Ireland's only producer of single malt.) A far bigger event is set to be marked with the bottling of Bushmills Millennium, a twenty-five-year-old whiskey for the new century. Bushmills' prospects for success look set to continue.

Bushmills
16 Year Old
Three Wood

*Old Bushmills Distillery,
Bushmills, Co. Antrim*

TYPE
Single malt

BOTTLING AGE
16 years

STRENGTH
40%

TASTE RATING
2

MINIATURES
Yes

COMMENTS
Full-bodied, malty with sweet, sherried overtones, this whiskey is unique in that it is matured in three different types of wooden casks.

VISITORS

Visitors are welcome 0900–1730 Mon.–Sat., 1200–1730 Sun. Apr.–Oct.; Nov.–Mar. Mon.–Fri. five tours daily at 1030, 1130, 1330, 1430, 1530.

*A*lthough it was only one of many distilleries in an area which was also famous for its abundant poteen production, Bushmills has emerged as the region's only survivor. Despite a few close calls, the company has been able to rely at crucial moments on some sound commercial judgement and plain old good luck to see it through the difficult times – as, for example, in the ending of Prohibition in the US, when buoyant stock levels allowed Bushmills to reap the rewards after the difficulties had ended. Its increasingly strong trading position saw it benefit from industry rationalization in the second half of the twentieth century, as in its gradual swallowing-up of the operations of Coleraine Distillery, and it has emerged from its amalgamations with the promise of a secure future.

Carolans

T. J. Carolan & Son Ltd,
Clonmel, Co. Tipperary

TYPE
Cream liqueur

STRENGTH
17%

TASTE RATING
2

MINIATURES
Yes

COMMENTS
A pleasantly smooth, honeyed, toffee-sweet Irish whiskey and spirit liqueur.

VISITORS
The plant is not open to visitors.

*F*irst launched in 1978, Carolans is another Irish success story and second only to Baileys in the world Irish cream liqueur market. T. J. Carolan & Son is now owned by C&C International, the Dublin-based wines and spirits group who own, among others, Tullamore Dew whiskey and Irish Mist liqueur. The company also produces Carolans Light, lower in fat and alcoholic content (at 15% abv) than the original, and Carolans Irish Coffee Cream, a newer brand produced especially for the North American market.

Finest Quality

COLERAINE

iRish whiskey

DISTILLED
BLENDED AND BOTTLED BY
THE OLD BUSHMILLS DISTILLERY CO. LTD.
BUSHMILLS CO. ANTRIM

40% vol   pRoduce of iReland   700 ml e

Coleraine

Old Bushmills Distillery,
Bushmills, Co. Antrim

TYPE
Blend

STRENGTH
40%

TASTE RATING
2

MINIATURES
No

COMMENTS
A fresh, light, sweet blend with a pleasantly rounded character.

VISITORS
Coleraine Distillery is no longer operational, but visitors are welcome at Old Bushmills, where Coleraine whiskey is produced, Visitors are welcome 0900– 1730 Mon.–Sat., 1200––1730 Sun. Apr.–Oct.; Nov.–Mar. Mon.–Fri. five tours daily at 1030, 1130, 1330, 1430, 1530. Telephone 01265-731521.

*P*reviously one of the most respected of Ireland's distilleries, Coleraine fell victim to the decline and rationalisation of the Irish whiskey industry this century. Distilling had been going on in the Coleraine area since the early seventeenth century, although the distillery itself did not become operational until over two hundred years later. Its reputation was high in the later nineteenth century, to the extent that Coleraine supplied whiskey to the House of Commons, subsequently selling their product under the name of 'Old Irish HC'. But like so many Irish distilleries, Coleraine suffered badly in the twentieth century, eventually being bought by the owners of Bushmills. Production continued very intermittently, latterly in grain whiskey, until closure came in 1978.

Connemara

Cooley Distillery,
Dundalk, Co. Louth

TYPE
Single malt

STRENGTH
40%

TASTE RATING
2–3

MINIATURES
No

COMMENTS
A drier single malt than Tyrconnell, its sister from the Cooley stable, this is a smooth, medium-bodied whiskey. Its soft and unassertive peaty flavour betrays its unique position as Ireland's only peated single malt.

VISITORS
Cooley Distillery is not open to visitors. However, visitors are welcome to Locke's Distillery Museum at Kilbeggan 0900–1800 daily, Apr.–Oct., 1000–1600 Nov.–Mar. Groups please telephone in advance; tel: 0506-32134.

Launched in 1996, Connemara is one of the newest brands from the forward-looking young Cooley Distillery, which began production in 1989. Formerly Ceimici Teo Distillery, it was bought in 1987 by entrepreneur John Teeling who had been keen for several years to enter the whiskey market. The takeover by Pernod Ricard of the Irish Distillers Group in the same year meant that by the time the Cooley Distillery whiskies came of age in 1992 after their required three-year maturation period, they offered the sole alternative to the Pernod/IDG monopoly. The Cooley whiskies are shipped by road to mature in oak-cask-filled warehouses at the old Locke's Distillery buildings in Kilbeggan, Co. Westmeath.

Crested Ten

*Midleton Distillery,
Midleton, Co. Cork*

TYPE

Blend

STRENGTH

40%

TASTE RATING

2

MINIATURES

No

COMMENTS

A smooth, easy-to-drink Irish blend with an unassertive dryness to complement its sweeter, malty notes.

VISITORS

Visitors are welcome to The Old Jameson Distillery, Bow St, Dublin and to the Old Midleton Distillery at Midleton, Co. Cork. Both are open 0930–1730 Mon.–Sun., all year. Telephone The Old Jameson Distillery on 01 8072355 and The Old Midleton Distillery on 021 613594.

A Jameson whiskey, Crested Ten is produced at the huge Midleton Distillery in Co. Cork where the Dublin company moved from their premises in the capital in 1975. By then, their old distillery at Bow Street – which once held over a million gallons of whiskey maturing in its honeycomb of cellars below the streets – had become too cramped. Today, over a dozen different whiskies, each with its own unique and individual character, are produced side-by-side in the remarkable Midleton Distillery.

The Dubliner

The Dubliner Liqueur &
Spirit Co., Dublin

TYPE
Cream liqueur

STRENGTH
17%

TASTE RATING
2

MINIATURES
No

COMMENTS
A relatively late addition to the Irish cream liqueur market, The Dubliner is a smooth, mellow chocolate-cream liqueur.

VISITORS
The plant is not open to visitors

*T*he Dubliner is the newest arrival to the Baileys family of Irish cream liqueurs, the biggest-selling cream liqueurs group in the world. It is produced, together with Emmets and O'Darby, in the company's plant at Bailieboro, Co. Cavan.

Dunphy's

Midleton Distillery,
Midleton, Co. Cork

TYPE
Blend

STRENGTH
40%

TASTE RATING
1

MINIATURES
No

COMMENTS

Blended especially for the export market and for mixing, this is a lighter-bodied Irish with a crisp, fresh palate and slightly spiritous finish.

*P*roduced for the first time in the 1950s, Dunphy's blend was dreamed up by a marketing department at Cork Distilleries Co. quick to capitalise on the contemporary fashion, notably in the US, for Irish coffee (with whiskey). The result was a blend meant to complement its co-ingredients, and not to taste too overpowering. Dunphy's has since been withdrawn from the US market, but is still produced at Midleton Distillery, primarily for home consumption.

VISITORS

Visitors are welcome to The Old Midleton Distillery at Midleton, Co. Cork. 0930–1730 Mon.–Sun., Mar.–Oct.; 1200–1500 Mon.–Sun., Nov.–Feb. Telephone 021 613594.

Eblana

*Cooley Distillery,
Dundalk, Co. Louth*

TYPE
Liqueur

STRENGTH
40%

TASTE RATING
2

MINIATURES
No

COMMENTS
A relative newcomer to the Irish drinks scene, Eblana is an ideal after-dinner liqueur with a rich texture and creamy, nutty-sweet flavours.

VISITORS
Cooley Distillery is not open to visitors. However, visitors are welcome to Locke's Distillery Museum at Kilbeggan 0900–1800 daily, Apr.–Oct., 1000–1600 Nov.–Mar. Groups please telephone in advance; telephone 0506-32134.

*A*dam Millar & Co. was an old name in Dublin distilling, first established in 1843 and based near the Guinness brewery on the Liffey's south bank. Their whiskey was popular throughout Ireland, and particularly in Dublin, from the earlier part of the twentieth century right up to the 1970s. Adam Millar was bought over by the Cooley Distillery and in 1994, Eblana was launched under the Millar label (Eblana being an ancient Irish name for Dublin). It won the Bronze Medal at the 1999 International Wine and Spirits Competition in London.

Emmets

R. & J. Emmet & Co.,
Dublin

TYPE
Cream liqueur

STRENGTH
17%

TASTE RATING
2

MINIATURES
No

COMMENTS
Emmets is a creamy, sweet and gently whiskied liqueur with chocolate and toffee flavours and a gentle, mellow finish.

VISITORS
The plant is not open to visitors.

*A*nother liqueur offering from the Gilbey's stable who produce several of the foremost Irish cream liqueurs, including Sheridans and Dubliner, and whose R. & A. Bailey subsidiary manufacture the eponymous top-selling liqueur. Emmets had previously been a stablemate of O'Darby, another cream liqueur, and Gilbey's parent company, International Distillers and Vintners Ltd (IDV) acquired both in 1991, confirming their dominant position in the cream liqueurs market. Emmets is named after Irish patriot and United Irishman Robert Emmet who was executed in 1803 after leading an unsuccessful revolt against British rule.

Green Spot

Mitchell & Son, Dublin

TYPE

Pot still

STRENGTH

40%

TASTE RATING

3

MINIATURES

No

COMMENTS

A traditional whiskey and, apart from at Mitchell's premises in Kildare St, it is hard to find. It is rich and complex and characterized by bags of typical pot-still character.

Distilled by John Jameson & Son, Green Spot pot-still whiskey has been produced by Dublin wine and spirit merchants Mitchell & Son for over eighty years. It is the only brand still produced specifically for an independent wine merchant in Ireland to sell under its own name, and the only one remaining from a range of 'coloured spot' whiskies formerly marketed by Mitchell's, a family-run firm which has been in business since 1805. The Kildare Street firm is now unique in Dublin, being the capital's last remaining wine merchant's shop.

Hewitts

*Midleton Distillery,
Midleton, Co. Cork*

TYPE
Blend

STRENGTH
40%

TASTE RATING
2–3

MINIATURES
No

COMMENTS
This is a rich blend whose nutty and malty flavours are overlain by a lighter, fragrant sweetness. It is a difficult-to-find brand.

VISITORS
Visitors are welcome to The Old Midleton Distillery at Midleton, Co. Cork. 0930–1730 Mon.–Sun., Mar.–Oct.; 1200–1500 Mon.–Sun., Nov.–Feb. Telephone 021 613594.

*H*ewitts whiskey commemorates the name of a founder of a family-owned Cork distillery which began production in the late eighteenth century. The company was one of the five south-western distilleries who joined together to form the Cork Distillers Co. in 1866 in an effort to take on the might and commercial dominance of the Dublin whiskey companies, most notably Jameson and Power. When the Irish Distilleries Group was formed in 1966, the former rivals came together under the one flag, and the distillery stopped making its grain whiskey in 1975. Hewitts is one of the smaller brands produced by the IDG complex at Midleton.

Inishowen

Cooley Distillery,
Dundalk, Co. Louth

TYPE

Blend

STRENGTH

40%

TASTE RATING

2

MINIATURES

No

COMMENTS

The newly revived Inishowen is a smooth, easy-to-drink blend with a refreshing gentle peatiness.

VISITORS

Cooley Distillery is not open to visitors. However, visitors are welcome to Locke's Distillery Museum at Kilbeggan 0900–1800 daily, Apr.–Oct., 1000–1600 Nov.–Mar. Groups please telephone in advance; tel: 0506-32134.

*W*ith the launch in 1996 of Inishowen, the independent Cooley Distillery has continued its practice of reviving old and respected names from the past of the Irish whiskey industry. Like Tyrconnell, Inishowen was originally a brand of the Londonderry distillery of A. A. Watt & Co., who traced their commercial origins back to the mid eighteenth century. But Watt's was one of the companies hard hit by US Prohibition in the 1920s, giving the Scottish DCL conglomerate the opportunity to buy out then close down a rival distillery. The company continued to trade only as a blenders until 1970, but its remaining assets were later merged with the new Cooley Distillery company.

Irish Mist

Irish Mist Liqueur Co.,
Tullamore, Co. Offaly

TYPE
Liqueur
STRENGTH
35%
TASTE RATING
2
MINIATURES
Yes

COMMENTS

A smooth and mellow blend of whiskies, fragrant herbs and an exotic heather honey.

VISITORS

A new Tullamore Dew visitors' centre is due to open in Spring 2000.

One of the longest-lasting and most successful liqueurs on the market, Irish Mist is owned by Dublin-based C&C International, whose other brands include Tullamore Dew whiskey and Carolans cream liqueur. It drew on the centuries-old notion of an Irish heather wine drunk in medieval times and was produced at Tullamore Distillery in 1947. The distillery, in common with others in Ireland, was in financial difficulties at the time and eventually closed in 1963. Irish Mist is today produced in Clonmel. Ownership of Tullamore and its products passed first to Irish Distillers then, in 1993, to C&C International.

Jameson

*Midleton Distillery,
Midleton, Co. Cork*

TYPE
Blend

STRENGTH
40%

TASTE RATING
2

MINIATURES
Yes

COMMENTS
Jameson's has a mellow sweetness balanced by fresher, floraly notes. Regarded by many as the classic of its type, this is the leading brand of Irish whiskey worldwide and the fastest growing brand internationally.

VISITORS
Visitors are welcome to The Old Jameson Distillery, Bow St, Dublin and to the Old Midleton Distillery at Midleton, Co. Cork. Both are open 0930–1730 Mon.–Sun., all year. Telephone 01 8072355 (Dublin) and 021 613594 (Midleton).

The arrival in Ireland of Scot John Jameson in the 1770s marked a significant new departure for the growing legal Irish whiskey industry. Jameson already had connections with the Scottish industry – he had even married into the Haig family – and his son consolidated the business by marrying a daughter of John Stein, whose family who were among the biggest grain distillers in Scotland and who owned Dublin's Bow Street distillery which Jameson Senior was soon to purchase. His exacting standards and aptitude for the business helped build his firm in the eighteenth century and into the nineteenth. Although own-label sales were still a concept of the future, Jameson's whiskey, sold through merchants, acquired the reputation, with Power's, of being the best of Irish.

Jameson Distillery Reserve

Midleton Distillery, Midleton, Co. Cork

TYPE	
Blend	
BOTTLING AGE	
12 years	
STRENGTH	
40%	
TASTE RATING	
3	
MINIATURES	
No	

COMMENTS

A rich, smooth and sherried whiskey with some complementary dry notes in its finish. Distillery Reserve can only be bought at Midleton Distillery.

VISITORS

Visitors are welcome to The Old Jameson Distillery, Bow St, Dublin 0930–1730 Mon.–Sun., all year. Telephone 01 8072355.

J ameson's successes in the nineteenth century were threatened, along with the fortunes of Irish whiskey in general, by an inability to recognise both the threat and the commercial possibilities offered by blending their pure whiskies with grain, a practice which was being adopted enthusiastically and successfully in Scotland. Yet more ground was lost during and after the Prohibition era in the US to the extent that, until surprisingly recently, Jameson's was a product known by few outside Ireland. Happily, that situation was remedied in part by the formation of the Irish Distillers Group, in which the firm was a key player. IDG's takeover by Pernod Ricard has further boosted Jameson's market presence.

Jameson
1780

*Midleton Distillery,
Midleton, Co. Cork*

TYPE

De luxe

BOTTLING AGE

12 years

STRENGTH

40%

TASTE RATING

3

MINIATURES

No

COMMENTS

An elegant whiskey of superior
character and a soothingly
mellow, sherried flavour. In
taste and qualities, not unlike
the Distillery Reserve. Visitors
are welcome to The Old
Jameson Distillery, Bow St,

VISITORS

Dublin and to the Old
Midleton Distillery at Midleton, Co. Cork. Both are open
0930–1730 Mon.–Sun., all year.
Telephone 01 8072355 (Dublin)
and 021 613594 (Midleton).

*B*y the time the Irish Distillers
Group was formed by
Jameson's, Power's and the Cork
Distilleries Co. in 1966, the Dublin
whisky companies were already out-
growing their cramped city-centre
premises. The decision to concentrate
production at Midleton in Co. Cork
saw all the partners eventually move
to a new, purpose-built plant there.
Today, over a dozen different
whiskies, each with their own unique
and individual character, are
produced side-by-side at this remarkable distillery. Jameson's, the world's
favourite Irish whiskey, is one of the
star performers in the Midleton
line-up. The whiskey's '1780' label
refers to the year of Jameson's foundation.

John's Lane

John's Lane Distillery,
Dublin

TYPE
Single-distillery Irish whiskey

BOTTLING AGE
Varies

STRENGTH
Varies

TASTE RATING
3

MINIATURES
Yes

COMMENTS
A medium-bodied whiskey with drier accents offsetting its more fragrant, sweeter flavours.

John's Lane Distillery was owned by the Power family, one of Dublin's two big distilling empires. The company was founded in 1791 by James Power, a local inn-keeper who, with his son, built the business rapidly, moving into their new distillery at John's Lane at the start of the new century. Their success was such that, from an initial output of a few thousand gallons a year, production grew to over 300,000 gallons by the 1830s. Not surprisingly the distillery itself was also rebuilt, eventually occupying a seven-acre site by the south side of the Liffey. But harsher times in the twentieth century brought contraction and, ultimately, merger into the Irish Distillers Group in 1966. The John's Lane site was abandoned, and production moved to the IDG plant at Midleton in the 1970s.

Jones Road

*Jones Road Distillery,
Dublin*

TYPE
Single-distillery Irish whiskey

BOTTLING AGE
Varies

STRENGTH
Varies

TASTE RATING
4

MINIATURES
Yes

COMMENTS
This is a robust, full-bodied whiskey with floral-spicy notes in its sweet flavour, counter-balanced by a powerful dryness.

Established 1842
CADENHEAD'S
AUTHENTIC
COLLECTION
150th anniversary commemoration
Irish Whiskey

This whiskey has been bottled from a selected individual cask in its natural state and shows the character of that cask. It has not been diluted with water. It has not been treated to change its colour and is free from all additives. It has not been subjected to any filtration that might remove natural constituents and spoil its flavour. It is the authentic product of its Distillery.

Bottled by Wm. Cadenhead, 32 Union Street, Campbeltown, SCOTLAND

From the   No.
JONES ROAD
Dublin Whiskey Distillery
Distilled in 1942 and bottled in 1991
Matured in an oak cask
750ml   for 48 years. 66.5%alc/vol

*J*ones Road Distillery, one of the few non-family whiskey companies in the capital, was established in the 1870s by a group of Dublin entrepreneurs who together formed the Dublin Whiskey Distillery Co. But a glut in the Dublin market meant that by 1889 the company had to merge with two of its city rivals, George Rowe and William Jameson, to form the Dublin Distilling Co. Although resources were pooled, each company produced its own whiskey for a time, but inauspicious trading conditions for Irish whiskey meant that operations were gradually run down in the three distilleries. Jones Road was finally closed in the 1940s.

Kilbeggan

*Cooley Distillery,
Dundalk, Co. Louth*

TYPE
Blend

STRENGTH
40%

TASTE RATING
2

MINIATURES
Yes

COMMENTS
Pleasant, clean and slightly sweet, this is a smooth blend with across-the-board appeal.

VISITORS
Cooley Distillery is not open to visitors. However, visitors are welcome to Locke's Distillery Museum at Kilbeggan 0900–1800 daily, Apr.–Oct., 1000–1600 Nov.–Mar. Groups please telephone in advance; tel: 0506-32134.

*L*ike its stablemates Locke's, Tyrconnell and Inishowen, Kilbeggan was already a famous name before its recent relaunch by Cooley Distillery. The original whiskey was named after the village where Locke's Distillery stood, and in Gaelic meant 'little church' – a reference to a local medieval monastery. It is an apposite name for a whiskey, as monks were always the foremost distillers in every country across Europe. With the collective difficulties facing the Irish whiskey industry in the twentieth century, Locke's Distillery barely survived into the 1950s. But with the whiskies of the Cooley Distillery, the old Locke names and reputations are being revived, the warehouses once again hold maturing stocks and the distillery itslef is being restored as a museum of industrial archaeology.

Locke's

Cooley Distillery,
Dundalk, Co. Louth

TYPE

Single Malt

STRENGTH

40%

TASTE RATING

2–3

MINIATURES

Yes

COMMENTS

Locke's is a smooth, full-flavoured whiskey, whose malty sweetness is complemented by dryer, fresher notes with a hint of peat.

VISITORS

Cooley Distillery is not open to visitors. However, visitors are welcome to Locke's Distillery Museum at Kilbeggan 0900–1800 daily, Apr.–Oct., 1000–1600 Nov.–Mar. Groups please telephone in advance; tel: 0506-32134

*A*nother revival from Cooley, Locke's was named after the nineteenth-century family-run distillery company. Licensed distilling began at the Kilbeggan site in 1757, and John Locke took over operations in 1843. The company remained successfully in business for over a century but by 1958, in common with much of Ireland's whiskey industry, receivership beckoned. After housing several business ventures the distillery came under the care of a local group until 1987, when the Locke company name was revived by the Cooley Distillery company who refurbished the warehouse and set up a cooperage. The old buildings are still being restored, and with equipment dating from Victorian times, the distillery itself is now a museum of industrial archaeology.

Midleton
Very Rare

*Midleton Distillery,
Midleton, Co. Cork*

TYPE

Blend

STRENGTH

40%

TASTE RATING

3–4

MINIATURES

No

COMMENTS

The flavour emphasis of individual years varies, but the whiskey is characteristically smooth, with a nutty fruit sweetness and counterbalancing dry notes.

VISITORS

Visitors are welcome to The Old Jameson Distillery, Bow St, Dublin and to the Old Midleton Distillery at Midle-ton, Co. Cork. Both are open 0930–1730 Mon.–Sun., all year. Telephone 01 8072355 (Dublin) and 021 613594 (Midleton).

*T*his whiskey is unusual in that it has been bottled annually since 1984, and each bottling is an event, limited to only several thousand individually numbered bottles. Distilling has been carried on at Midleton since 1825, when it was first established by the Murphy brothers (another branch of whose family began a brewery in Cork, still going strong). In 1868 the distillery joined the newly formed conglomerate of Cork Distilleries Co. and, almost a century later, the Irish Distillers Group. It survived the upheaval of both mergers, emerging as the single most important whiskey-production centre in Ireland. Over a dozen whiskies of varying traditions, tastes and characthers are produced there, a testimony to the skill of its craftspeople.

Millars
Special Reserve

Cooley Distillery,
Dundalk, Co. Louth

TYPE

Blend

STRENGTH

40%

TASTE RATING

2–3

MINIATURES

No

COMMENTS

A smooth, nicely balanced blend which is sweet and fruity on the nose and in its flavours, with a complementary pleasing dryness.

VISITORS

Cooley Distillery is not open to visitors. However, visitors are welcome to Locke's Distillery Museum at Kilbeggan 0900–1800 daily, Apr.–Oct., 1000–1600 Nov.–Mar. Groups please telephone in advance; tel: 0506-32134.

*A*dam Millar & Co. was an old name in Dublin distilling, first established in 1843 and based near the Guinness brewery on the Liffey's south bank, and their whiskey was popular in Ireland, and particularly in Dublin, from the earlier part of the twentieth century right up to the 1970s. Adam Millar was bought over by the Cooley Distillery who have now relaunched Millars Special Reserve whiskey. Although on the market only since 1994, it is already an award winner. Eblana, a whiskey liqueur, was also launched under the Millar label, Eblana being an ancient Irish name for Dublin.

Millwood

PR Nederlands Spirits & Wines B.V., Groupe Pernod Ricard, Tilburg, The Netherlands

TYPE

Cream liqueur

STRENGTH

17%

TASTE RATING

2

MINIATURES

No

COMMENTS

Millwoods is a pleasant, non-cloying liqueur with chocolatey background flavours.

*P*R Nederland Spirits & Wines, B.V., had substantial expertise in the liqueurs market with their advocaat brands before launching Millwood in 1980. It is made with fresh Dutch cream, smooth Irish whiskey and good quality Irish spirits. It has a low fat content which gives it a light and velvety texture. Millwod has enjoyed considerable success in international competition and is distributed in over 65 countries worldwide.

O'Darby

J. J. O'Darby Ltd,
Dublin

TYPE

Cream liqueur

STRENGTH

17%

TASTE RATING

2

MINIATURES

No

COMMENTS

A mellow, caramel-sweet blend of Irish whiskey and spirits with cream and chocolate.

VISITORS

The plant is not open to visitors.

*A*nother of the Irish cream liqueurs to hit the market after the success of Baileys, O'Darby was originally made by a small local company before being bought by rival producers R. & J. Emmet; they in turn were bought by International Distillers and Vintners subsidiary Gilbey's in 1991. Emmets and The Dubliner cream liqueurs are produced alongside O'Darby, but the expertise at their Bailieboro plant means that the distinctive character and individual flavours of each brand is not only never compromised, but enhanced.

Paddy

TYPE

Blend

STRENGTH

40%

TASTE RATING

2

MINIATURES

Yes

COMMENTS

Paddy is light and fresh, almost sharp in its flavours, with a dry finish.

VISITORS

Visitors are welcome to The Old Midleton Distillery at Midleton, Co. Cork. 0930–1730 Mon.–Sun., Mar.–Oct.; 1200– 1500 Mon.–Sun., Nov.–Feb. Telephone 021 613594.

*T*raditionally a Cork whiskey, Paddy is still the favoured brand of the south-west. It is now made by the Irish Distillers Group but its original owners were proclaimed in its unwieldy title, 'Cork Distilleries Company Old Irish Whiskey', a name which did not exactly flow from the tongue, or pen. In the 1910s the name began to be abandoned by Cork drinkers and publicans in favour of 'Paddy Flaherty's whiskey' – after an ebullient local rep. The full name eventually made its way onto the label, first at the foot then, simply as 'Paddy', as its main name. Cork Distilleries Co., themselves the result of an 1867 merger of a number of local distilleries, merged in 1966 into IDG, with their distillery at Midleton the one chosen as the group's production centre.

Power's

*Midleton Distillery,
Midleton, Co. Cork*

TYPE
Blend

STRENGTH
40%

TASTE RATING
3

MINIATURES
Yes

COMMENTS
A fresh, smooth Irish with fruity and malt flavours and a dry finish. This is the most popular of all Irish whiskies on the home market.

VISITORS
Visitors are welcome to The Old Midleton Distillery at Midleton, Co. Cork. 0930–1730 Mon.–Sun., Mar.–Oct.; 1200–1500 Mon.–Sun., Nov.–Feb. Telephone 021 613594.

*B*egun in 1791, Power & Son were one of the most far-sighted and successful Irish distillers of the nineteenth century. The company was responsible for some impressive marketing innovations, helping shape the whiskey market to a state recognisable today. In 1886 they became pioneers of bottling (then almost all drinks were sold from the barrel), protecting their product from adulteration, enhancing their name and emphasising their distinctiveness with the addition of a gold label still used on their whiskey today. Bottling also expanded the market by making whiskey portable to the home. Another first came with Powers' introduction of the miniature to the Irish market: a bottle had three swallows' capacity, and a celebratory visual pun is still seen on Powers' labels today.

Redbreast

Midleton Distillery, Midleton, Co. Cork

TYPE	Pot still
BOTTLING AGE	12 years
STRENGTH	40%
TASTE RATING	3
MINIATURES	No

COMMENTS

*J*ameson's whiskies are the ones traditionally associated with this twelve years old, pure pot still Irish brand. It was first launched in 1939 for sale to whiskey merchants, but after Jameson's merger in 1966 into the Irish Distillers Group and subsequent move to Midleton Distillery in Co. Cork, stocks for Redbreast were no longer forthcoming. However, IDG recently decided to relaunch the brand themselves, through their Dublin-based vintners subsidiary Fitzgerald & Co. They are based in the IDG headquarters at Bow Street, in part of the old Jameson's distillery.

Redbreast is a classically Irish whiskey with an abundance of smooth, pot-still character. A difficult whiskey to find, even in Ireland.

VISITORS

Visitors are welcome to The Old Midleton Distillery at Midleton, Co. Cork. 0930–1730 Mon.–Sun., Mar.–Oct.; 1200–1500 Mon.–Sun., Nov.–Feb. Telephone 021 613594.

Royal Irish

Royal Irish Distillery,
Belfast

TYPE

Single distillery Irish malt

STRENGTH

Varies

TASTE RATING

3

MINIATURES

Yes

COMMENTS

A difficult-to-find whiskey sold only by independent bottlers, whose sweet, fragrant taste has counterbalancing drier notes and a pot-still backdrop.

Owned by the Dunville family, Belfast spirits merchants who decided to move into the whiskey-producing side of the business, the Royal Irish Distillery was built in 1869. Its products acquired a fine reputation, and the company's fortunes rode high in the late nineteenth and early twentieth century. The distillery also had the distinction of having its own, national-league-winning football team. But in the 1930s, having weathered the storms of domestic strife, US Prohibition and a world-wide depression, the company suffered a body-blow in the premature death of the last of the Dunville family. Rather than pursue an agressive sales approach to win new markets, the rest of the board voted to dissolve the company. Distilling resumed for only a brief period in the 1950s.

Sheridan's

Thomas Sheridan & Sons, Dublin

TYPE

Cream liqueur

STRENGTH

17% (vanilla cream), 19.5% (coffee chocolate liqueur)

TASTE RATING

2

MINIATURES

No

COMMENTS

*V*isually stunning both on the shelf and in the glass, this award-winning cream liqueur is one of the most imaginative drinks ever produced. Not surprisingly, it is also the foremost impulse-buy in the drinks market as a whole. Thomas Sheridan & Sons is owned by the Gilbey's group which produces, among others, Baileys, the world's top selling liqueur. Like its stablemate, it is produced at the company's plant in Dublin, but unlike Baileys, Sheridan's was an instant success when it was launched on the cream liqueur market in early 1994. Sheridan's apparent gimmickry should not blind purchasers to the fact that this is a seriously good liqueur.

Its white liqueur has a soothing, white-chocolate richness, the black warming coffee and whiskey flavours and a rounded, chocolatey-nutty finish. The whole is smooth and elegant, akin to a deliciously whiskied liquid *tiramisù*.

VISITORS

The plant is not open to visitors.

Tullamore

Tullamore Distillery,
Tullamore, Co. Offaly

TYPE
Single-distillery Irish whiskey

BOTTLING AGE
Varies

STRENGTH
Varies

TASTE RATING
3

MINIATURES
Yes

COMMENTS
A typically light but not spiritous whiskey with a fragrant,
sweet flavour.

Established 1842

CADENHEAD'S
AUTHENTIC
COLLECTION
150th anniversary commemoration
Irish Whiskey

This whiskey has been bottled from a selected individual cask
in its natural state and shows the character of that cask.
It has not been diluted with water. It has not been treated to
change its colour and is free from all additives. It has
not been subjected to any filtration that might remove
natural constituents and spoil its flavour.
It is the authentic product of its Distillery.

Bottled by Wm. Cadenhead, 32 Union Street, Campbeltown,
SCOTLAND

From
DALY's   No.
TULLAMORE DISTILLERY
Distilled in 1949 and bottled in 1991
Matured in an oak cask
750ml   for **41** years.   65.6%alc/vol

*T*ullamore Distillery was founded in 1829, well placed in the
Midlands for distributing its produce
via the Grand Canal. Throughout its
history the distillery has been
renowned for producing the lightest
and most accessible of Irish whiskies,
a tradition carried on today. But with
the rest of the industry in Ireland,
Tullamore died a slow death into the
mid twentieth century. Its decline was
offset by the success of its Irish Mist
liqueur, but the distillery, still with
plenty of stocks, closed in 1954. Since
then it has been gradually demolished. Its products were bought by
Power & Son in 1965, passing with it
the following year into the Irish
Distillers Group. In 1994 the business
was sold on again to C&C
Intenational, part of Allied Domecq.

Tullamore Dew

Tullamore Dew Co. Ltd,
Tullamore, Co. Offaly

TYPE

Blend

STRENGTH

40%

TASTE RATING

2

MINIATURES

Yes

COMMENTS

A light, undemanding Irish blend with a smooth, sweet flavour. Good as an aperitif.

VISITORS

A new Tullamore Dew visitors' centre is due to open in Spring 2000.

*T*ullamore Distillery closed in 1963, but the name of its most famous whiskey lives on in a new incarnation which is one of the most popular Irish whiskies in Europe. The distillery was originally founded in 1829 by Michael Molloy, but by the late 1880s was under the co-ownership and control of Daniel E. Williams, who had worked at the distillery from his boyhood. His initials were the inspiration for the name of the company's most famous product and, in turn, for the deathless advertising slogan 'Give Every Man His Dew'. The distillery fell victim to the recession in the Irish whiskey industry in the mid twentieth century, and today Tullamore Dew is produced in Co. Cork at Midleton Distillery.

Tyrconnell

Cooley Distillery,
Dundalk, Co. Louth

TYPE

Single malt

STRENGTH

40%

TASTE RATING

2–3

MINIATURES

Yes

COMMENTS

The Tyrconnell is smooth, mellow whiskey whose light and sweet taste is complemented by a pleasingly dry finish.

VISITORS

Cooley Distillery is not open to visitors. However, visitors are welcome to Locke's Distillery Museum at Kilbeggan 0900–1800 daily, Apr.–Oct., 1000–1600 Nov.–Mar. Groups please telephone in advance; tel: 0506-32134.

*T*oday produced at the Cooley Distillery, this whiskey was once the prime brand of the Londonderry distillery of A. A. Watt & Co., which was bought out and closed by the Scottish Distillers Company Ltd in 1925. The original Tyrconnell was one of the most popular Irish whiskies in the early twentieth century, and was therefore a fitting candidate for revival recently by its new owners, John Locke & Co. In 1876 the name Tyrconnell was borne by a horse which was owned by the Watt family and entered in the Irish classic race, 'The Queen Victoria Plate'. The horse's victory and its dream odds are still celebrated on its namesake's label today.

Appendix 1:
Developing the Palate
by Una Holden-Cosgrove

*A*part from the anatomical meaning – the roof of the mouth – a palate refers to the sense of taste, but the roof of the mouth does play an important role in discerning a taste. Spicy, hot and cold, pleasant and objectionable sensations are all in the province of the palate. Everyone has a different reaction to taste and both physically and psychologically the sense of smell has a major influence on how these sensations are perceived.

Where whisky is concerned, a palate needs to be educated in the same way as it must gradually be introduced to the different foods encountered in different countries – after all, a vindaloo is hardly the best introduction to curries! Similarly, a dram of one whisky can never be regarded as a real experience or a satisfactory introduction to the elixir of life. Every whisky has a different taste and smell: some are quite fierce, or vigorous, and others more honeyed and enticing. To attempt one of the more powerful malts, such as The Glenlivet or Talisker, without any previous knowledge of whisky can only kill any interest in proceeding further.

Unfortunately the early writers on whisky overlooked the fact that their palates were accustomed to the differing tastes and had been conditioned so that the robust types were more to their particular liking. As a result the malts and blends they recommended so highly were usually too powerful for the beginner, leading to an undeservedly macho image for malt whisky which meant that these stronger whiskies were more commonly found on the shelves of bars outside Scotland.

An ideal way to demonstrate this difference in taste is used at whisky-tasting sessions, where the participants are gently guided through a series of malts, starting with the softer, fruity smelling ones and slowly working through to the stronger ones. With this manipulation of the palate, almost invariably the participants find the final dram the most appealing! As these participants do not always appreciate that the aim of tastings is to show how good even the stronger malts are when the palate has been tutored, they are liable to seek out the strongest one to try again at a later date, only to find it tastes too strong – their palate has not really developed sufficiently to cope with it without more experience. So how should a palate be developed?

It is perhaps advisable to start with a whisky mix, as long as the whisky is a blend, or a grain such as Invergordon, and not a malt. Lemonade, soda, even water and ice are possible mixes for blended whisky. This will begin to train the senses and on cold days a Whisky Mac (blended whisky and Green Ginger) will provide a feeling of warmth that goes hand in hand with other pleasant sensations. A really fine blend – such as Black Bottle – can then be attempted neat.

Graduation to a malt requires good company and careful thought. For most beginners the spirit should not assail the taste buds, but inveigle the senses through an appealing scent, subtle taste and soothing after-effects. The aroma, which should be savoured before a sip is taken, can be spicy, fruity, flowery or peaty, and as with other scents like perfume and aftershave, individual preferences must be considered. The taste for the inexperienced should not be fierce – instead, the malt should be chosen from among the smooth, velvety and honeyed selections. Some are dry and others a little sweet, and once again personal preference must be recognized.

After-effects are every bit as important, as the palate can be attacked some time after a stronger malt has been imbibed, and this can be unpleasant to the unwary. There are a variety of exciting after-effects that should be experienced and appreciated. The sparkles on the tongue and roof of the mouth provided by such malts as Oban and Aberlour are quite delightful, the feeling of being massaged, not just in the mouth but all over the shoulders and back, as produced by such as Glendullan after only one sip will help to cure most stress reactions. There are sensations of glowing warmth in the mouth, further reminiscent tastes of fruit or other pleasant foods and even a very delayed sharpness that comes as an unexpected surprise.

The use of miniatures is extremely helpful in identifying whiskies that appeal most to an individual. Further tutoring of the palate should be by experiencing the stronger ones in graduated steps, rather than by assaulting an unprepared and unsuspecting mouth!

Very simply, to drink a malt whisky properly, in order to obtain maximum enjoyment, it is necessary to consider the smell, taste and after-effects that would appeal to a particular individual. Time should be spent appreciating the aroma, taking only a small sip, letting it roll around the mouth before swallowing it and then awaiting the enjoyment of its after-effects. It is also well to remember that mood and the time of day as well as the weather conditions play a role in palate appeal. What may at the end of a horrible day seem like the most wonderful malt on earth, could well appear boring and inadequate on a cold winter's night or overwhelming in the middle of a happy gathering on a glorious summer's afternoon. Remember, too, that a palate will change with experience.

There are many, many blends, a few grain whiskies, a number of vatted malts and about 160 single malts (from approximately 120 distilleries, with some producing more than one year and volume) from which to choose. All are different, each with a different effect on different palates and providing the customer with a wonderful choice and opportunity to learn about a fascinating topic. If the beginner treats whisky with respect, the experiences encountered in the process of development will prove enchanting.

Appendix 2:
Personal Tasting Record

All the whiskies featured in this book are listed below. As you try each one, record a mark out of 10, in terms of personal enjoyment according to your own tastes and preferences, and so build up a personalised tasting log.

Scotch

☐	Aberfeldy	☐	Ben Nevis
☐	Aberlour	☐	Benriach
☐	An Cnoc	☐	Benrinnes
☐	The Antiquary	☐	Benromach
☐	Ardbeg	☐	Black & White
☐	Ardmore	☐	Black Bottle
☐	Arran	☐	Black Watch
☐	Auchentoshan	☐	Bladnoch
☐	Aultmore	☐	Blair Athol
☐	Bailie Nicol Jarvie	☐	Bowmore
☐	Balblair	☐	Bruichladdich
☐	Ballentine's	☐	Bunnahabhain
☐	Balmenach	☐	Cameron Brig
☐	The Balvenie	☐	Caol Ila
☐	Banff	☐	Caperdonich
☐	Bell's Extra Special	☐	Cardhu

☐	Chivas Regal	☐	Fairlie's
☐	The Claymore	☐	The Famous Grouse
☐	Clynelish	☐	Fraser McDonald
☐	Coleburn	☐	Glayva
☐	Columba Cream	☐	Glen Albyn
☐	Convalmore	☐	Glenburgie
☐	Cragganmore	☐	Glencadam
☐	Craigellachie	☐	Glen Calder
☐	Crawford's 3-Star	☐	Glen Deveron
☐	Cutty Sark	☐	Glendronach
☐	Cutty Sark Emerald	☐	Glendullan
☐	Cutty Sark Imperial Kingdom Golden Jubilee	☐	Glenfarclas
☐	Dailuaine	☐	Glenfiddich
☐	The Dalmore	☐	Glen Garioch
☐	Dalwhinnie	☐	Glengoyne
☐	Deanston	☐	Glen Grant
☐	Dewar's White Label	☐	Glen Keith
☐	Dimple	☐	Glenkinchie
☐	Drambuie	☐	The Glenlivet
☐	Dufftown	☐	Glenlochy
☐	Dunhill Old Master	☐	Glenlossie
☐	Dunkeld Atholl Brose	☐	Glen Mhor
☐	Edradour	☐	Glenmorangie
		☐	Glenmorangie Port Wood

☐	Glen Moray	☐	J&B Jet
☐	Glen Ord	☐	Johnnie Walker Black Label
☐	Glen Rosa	☐	Johnnie Walker Blue Label
☐	The Glenrothes	☐	Johnnie Walker Red Label
☐	Glen Scotia	☐	Knockando
☐	Glentauchers	☐	Lagavulin
☐	The Glenturret	☐	Laphroaig
☐	The Glenturret Original Malt Liqueur	☐	Lauder's Scotch
☐	Glenugie	☐	Ledaig
☐	Grand Macnish	☐	Linkwood
☐	Grant's Family Reserve	☐	Littlemill
☐	Haig	☐	The Loch Fyne
☐	Heather Cream	☐	Loch Ranza
☐	Highland Park	☐	Lochside
☐	Immortal Memory	☐	Long John
☐	Imperial	☐	Longmorn
☐	Inchgower	☐	Longrow
☐	Inchmurrin	☐	The Macallan
☐	Invergordon	☐	Millburn
☐	Inverleven	☐	Miltonduff
☐	Islay Mist	☐	Mitchell's
☐	Isle of Jura	☐	Mortlach
☐	J&B Rare	☐	North Port
		☐	Oban

APPENDIX 2

	Old Fettercairn
	Old Parr
	Old Pulteney
	The Original Mackinlay
	Passport
	Pinwinnie
	Pittyvaich
	Port Ellen
	Pride of Islay
	Pride of the Lowlands
	Pride of Orkney
	Pride of Strathspey
	Rosebank
	Royal Brackla
	Royal Culross
	Royal Lochnagar
	St Magdalene
	Scapa
	Scotia Royale
	The Singleton of Auchroisk
	Speyburn
	Springbank
	Stag's Breath Liqueur

	Stewarts Cream of the Barley
	Strathisla
	Talisker
	The Talisman
	Tamdhu
	Tamnavulin
	Teacher's Highland Cream
	Teaninich
	Tobermory
	Tomatin
	Tomintoul
	The Tormore
	Tullibardine
	Ultima
	VAT 69
	Wallace
	White Horse
	Whyte & Mackay
	William Grant

Irish

- Baileys
- Black Bush
- Bow Street
- Bushmills
- Bushmills Distillery Reserve
- Bushmills 10 Years Old
- Bushmills 16 Years Old
- Carolans
- Coleraine
- Connemara Pure Pot Still
- Crested Ten
- The Dubliner
- Dunphys
- Eblana
- Emmets
- Green Spot
- Hewitt's
- Inishowen
- Irish Mist
- Jameson
- Jameson Distillery Reserve
- Jameson 1780
- John's Lane

- Jones Road
- Kilbeggan
- Locke's Single Malt
- Midleton Very Rare
- Millar's Special Reserve
- Millwood Cream
- O'Darby
- Paddy
- Power's
- Redbreast
- Royal Irish
- Sheridan's
- Tullamore
- Tullamore Dew
- Tyrconnell